INSTANT LOSS
eat real, lose weight

INSTANT LOSS

eat real, lose weight

BRITTANY WILLIAMS

PHOTOGRAPHY BY GHAZALLE BADIOZAMANI

HOUGHTON MIFFLIN HARCOURT

BOSTON   NEW YORK

Copyright © 2019 by Brittany Williams

Photography © 2019 by Ghazalle Badiozamani

Cross hatching pattern © Shutterstock/ Babich Alexander

Author family photos and personal before-and-after photos © 2019 by Brittany Williams

Fan photos © 2019 by Rebecca and Dan, Denise Caillouet, Hanna Nibbe, Melissa Bartholomew, Shawna Beam, Evelin Dittman, Kyra Stovall

Food styling by Monica Pierini

Prop styling by Jenna Tedesco

For information about permission to reproduce selections from this book, write to trade.permissions@hmhco.com or to Permissions, Houghton Mifflin Harcourt Publishing Company, 3 Park Avenue, 19th Floor, New York, New York 10016.

hmhbooks.com

Library of Congress Cataloging-in-Publication Data is available.

ISBN 978-0-358-12185-5 (pbk)

ISBN 978-0-358-12186-2 (ebk)

Book design by Suet Chong

Printed in Canada

FP 10 9 8 7 6 5 4 3 2

4500786956

For Avey, Ben, and Noah
My little ragtag bunch.
You are my reason.

contents

thank you

Brady, you're the real MVP. Thank you for supporting my dreams, encouraging me to create, and for doing countless loads of dishes. I love you crazy big.

Avey, Ben, and Noah, faithful taste testers, comedic relief, and lights of my life. Being your mother is my greatest accomplishment. Thank you for sharing me so that I can help others. I love you.

Mom and Dad, thank you for always being my #1 fans, for all the free babysitting, and for sharing your stories in this book. You are an inspiration!

Family, there are SO many of you, thank you all!! To my sister, Bethany, for all the encouragement, my Aunt Kim for all the free phone therapy, my grandparents (all of you) who have helped me in ways unspeakable, my brothers, Colin, Kyle, Connor, Caleb, and Tristan, for buying more books than any sane person/people should—I love you guys. There are too many of you to name, but you know who you are. I'm so grateful to have a mess of people who love me.

Friends Heather, Shaylee, Janna, AlinaJoy, Katie, Roxanne, Carol, Tracy, Teri, Samantha, Candy, Chrissy, and Tana—I'm forgetting people, but you know who you are. My dearest sisters, I am thankful that no matter how far life takes us apart, it brings us right back together without missing a step. Thank you for investing in me, even if it's just a text that I forget to respond to. Love you all.

My editor, Justin Schwartz, plus Sari Kamin, Brianna Yamashita, Jacqueline Quirk, Marina Padakis Lowry, Tai Blanche, designer Suet Chong, and the entire HMH team. This has been such a great experience. Thank you for listening to my vision and trusting me to take it where I wanted. You made me a better writer and developer by pushing my boundaries, just a bit, and the culmination of growth is shown here on these pages. I couldn't have asked for a better team of people. Justin, I just adore you, I hope you know.

My photography team—Ghazalle Badiozamani, Monica Pierini, Jenna Tedesco, Bridget Kenny, Leila Clifford, and Toby Klinger. I still can't get over how you looked at photos of my living room and created an entire photoshoot around them! Every single photo in this book is magnificent, and it was an honor to watch you ladies work. Thank you for sharing your talents. You elevated this project to another level.

Ashley Wright Photography, thank you for answering my panicked call and editing my family photos so they have that extra touch of brilliance. You are a brilliant photographer but an even better friend. If you're in DFW, look her up!

Lisa Rovick, for testing every. single. recipe. Thank you for the countless hours on the phone and all of your advice and expertise. These recipes are beyond because of you. I loved every second of working side by side in the kitchen with you, even if it was across the country.

My agent, Andrea Barzvi, at Empire Literary, you keep me sane. Thank you for sharing your wisdom, counsel, and for believing in me before most.

The Instant Loss Community, I wouldn't be here if it wasn't for you. You saw something in me before I ever saw it in myself. Not every girl has 150,000 friends that she gets to talk to every day! I'm so proud of the community we've built, designed to encourage and elevate others. I'm so grateful for how y'all really uplifted me. Thank you for contributing to the conversation. We are helping so many together, and I pray that we get to do so for a very long time.

Jesus, my story is full of broken pieces that You continuously help me put back together in the most meaningful ways. Thank you for being the grace that saved my life.

I asked my husband for a stovetop pressure cooker and he surprised me with this newfangled fancy machine with a million buttons instead. I was frustrated. I didn't want some technowiz gizmo gadget with a manual as long as my arm. I had two toddlers and another baby on the way. I didn't need another thing to figure out. I just wanted a regular old pressure cooker. The Instant Pot was no regular pressure cooker.

It sat in a box in our living room for weeks. I was intimidated and a bit scared I was going to blow up the house, so I let it sit there. Eventually it became part of the furniture. Couch, coffee table, arm chair, Instant Pot. One day, my husband asked me if he should return it. He got my guilty conscience all stirred up, and I finally took it out of the box.

I spent an entire morning reading the manual cover to cover. I figured I'd try my hand at making rice. Rice is cheap—if I mess it up, what have I lost?

In about half an hour, we had perfectly cooked rice. I didn't have to babysit it on the stove, I just threw all the ingredients in the pot, folded a couple loads of laundry, changed a diaper, and presto! Rice!

My kids asked for seconds. I was sold.

I've had my pot for three years. Since then, I've had three more pregnancies. My weight has yo-yoed along with my willpower.

In January 2017, I was sick and tired of feeling sick and tired. I kicked processed food and I stopped eating fast food. I was confident that, with the help of my pressure cooker, my family could successfully stop eating out and start eating most of our meals at home.

Well, we're doing it! I haven't asked my husband to bring home dinner at all this year! With the exception of a couple date nights, we haven't eaten anywhere but home for the last three months. As an awesome side effect, I've lost 41 pounds!

So, to my Instant Pot, thank you. I really love you and I think everyone should have you.

—Brittany Williams, Facebook post, April 3, 2017

preface

I n 2017, the post on the previous page went viral on Facebook. I received thousands of friend requests, private messages, and comments. Everyone wanted to know the same thing, "Do you have a cookbook? How can I do this too?" So I started the Instant Loss Facebook community out of pure necessity. Within 24 hours, we had over 20,000 people join. If there was something I was doing that could help other people, I wanted to share it. I began posting my recipes on Facebook, but it was inefficient. I needed an easier way to share recipes, so one week after that Facebook post of mine went crazy, I launched InstantLoss.com.

I was a homeschooling, stay-at-home mom of three who had no computer experience. I didn't know what I was doing. My website was paperclipped and duct-taped together. I honestly didn't think anyone would be interested in anything I had to say, but our first day online the site had 52,000 views!

People began making my recipes and started to see the pounds fall off. But the most encouraging thing for me was being able to witness the empowerment people were experiencing through befriending their kitchens and taking charge of what they were eating.

By the end of 2017, I'd lost 125 pounds and saw my

autoimmune disease go into remission, and I did it all through changing my relationship with food.

We had members in our community who were boasting the same success. It wasn't a diet, and we weren't restricting ourselves. Weight loss was a byproduct of fixing the real problem and we were all excited to share.

In 2018, we released the *Instant Loss Cookbook*. I was completely terrified. I didn't know if people would love or hate it. I was just a regular girl; a book was big time! I was working 12- to 16-hour days at that point, running Instant Loss, creating content, and developing recipes. I told my husband, if just one person reads the book and feels like they're not alone anymore, it'll all be worth it.

The book came out in October 2018 and was a smashing success. It became a national bestseller and crazy things started to happen! I was featured in the *New York Post* and invited to be on the *Today* show with Al Roker and Joy Bauer. People connected, and they loved the recipes, but everyone had one question, "When's the next book coming out?"

So, I gladly threw myself back into development mode and spent the majority of 2019 creating the book that you're holding in your hands. Though all of this required a lot of very hard work on my part, I am not disillusioned. I know exactly why I'm here and why I have experienced the amount of success I've experienced. I owe it all to you and to my Heavenly Father.

Y'all's support has propelled me to where I am today. It's enabled me to do what I'm passionate about for a living, and it drives me to continue to create. Never in my wildest dreams could I have

before

after

imagined when I wrote that Facebook post that two years later I'd be sitting here, a national bestselling author with her second book. I am only able to do all that I do because of your support. I never want to forget, trivialize, or take that for granted. From the bottom of my heart, I thank you.

In *Instant Loss Eat Real, Lose Weight,* you'll find over 100 recipes for your Instant Pot, air fryer, and more. The recipes are crazy delicious, most come together in under 30 minutes, and they've been tested and received the seal of approval from families just like yours!

Within the next few pages, you'll find more practical information on how I lost the weight and why I've been able to successfully keep it off for two years. I've also included an ingredient section that includes acceptable substitutions for those with allergies, so that no one has to feel left out.

This book is so different from my first. I attribute a lot of that to the team at my publisher, HMH, for taking this wild card on. One of the biggest gripes I heard with the first book was that there weren't enough photos. Because the team for this book is so incredible and believes in what we're doing, we were able to provide a stunning photo for almost every single recipe in the book. I wanted so many accompanying photos because I knew that they would help you tremendously as you cook your way through the book!

During this process, I've found that change can sometimes manifest itself almost instantly. Believing in myself and the wild possibility of my own impact has encouraged others to believe in themselves in the same way. To paraphrase something I read in a book once, sometimes someone has to show you how to love something before you can love it. It is my fervent wish that, by reading through these pages, you see my love for nutrition and might be encouraged to gain a new love and appreciation for nutrition yourself.

Wishing you wellness in all that you do,

Brittany

introduction

DITCH THAT DIET!

This isn't a diet book. This is a book about loving yourself, loving food, and experiencing freedom from the self-inflicted bondage we've all experienced in our pursuit of "skinny."

I've been on countless diets throughout the years, pursuing the wrong thing. The issue with dieting is that it's not sustainable. It teaches you the rules of the diet, but what happens next? How do you maintain the success you achieved? Or how do you continue to achieve success when the way you're eating is so restrictive that it's not something you want to continue for any length of time?

I want to encourage you to *stop* pursuing skinny. If weight loss is your main motivation, I'm going to share with you why that might be foiling your progress. I chased after this ideological image of myself for years in a relentless pursuit of being thin. If there was a diet, I tried it. A pill, I took it. But I was focusing on all the wrong things. My mind would tell me "if you were thin, you'd be happy." But my mind was wrong.

Healthy isn't a size.

Happiness isn't a weight.

My problem wasn't that I was obese. That was just a symptom. My problem was that I didn't hold myself in high enough regard. I didn't assign enough value to my health and well-being. I gave my time, effort, and sanity to everyone around me, never prioritizing my own needs. Then, after I was beaten down, with nothing left and exhausted to the depths of my soul, I'd medicate myself with food.

"You deserve this," I'd tell myself.

"You've earned this ice cream."

"A cheeseburger will make you feel all better."

I had to surrender my right to be led by my desires and acknowledge that my desires don't always have my best interests in mind. I was battling with disorder eating. Using food to self-medicate and "fix" the issues I had with myself, self-sabotaging all the while. Bingeing on junk food never fixed one of my problems, though it compounded a lot of them.

Maybe you don't have the same issue I had; maybe for you, it's simply not having the proper tools, which we'll get to. But if you, like me, have been chasing this version of yourself that you've never really been able to obtain, maybe it's time to stop chasing. Maybe it's time to acknowledge that you are perfectly enough right now, exactly as you are. Maybe it's time to acknowledge that your issues aren't because of a symptom but part of a bigger problem and you need to align yourself with the solution.

THE DIET DILEMMA

There are so many different diets out there, it's hard to know which one to choose. Is low-carb/high-fat the right way? High-protein/low-fat? It can be completely overwhelming and confusing when one week coconut oil is going to cure cancer, but the next week it's demonized for saturated fat. (Our cell membranes need saturated fat, by the way; after all, 50% of their composition is made up of saturated fatty acids.)

I'm convinced the reason there are so many different types of diets is because we're all so different. Some of us need more meat, and some do better with a pescatarian-style diet, while others thrive on a plant-based one. No matter what diet or belief system you ascribe to, there is one thing that everyone can agree on.

No one thrives on a processed food diet.

Books have been written and documentaries have been filmed. There have been personal trainers who stopped working out and started eating junk food just to prove this point. The human body wasn't designed to live on processed food alone. Weight gain is a mild issue compared to the debilitating illnesses a processed food diet can trigger: diabetes, high blood pressure, high cholesterol, autoimmune disease, fatty liver—the list goes on and on.

The best diet is the one that you can stick to for the rest of your life.

I used to roll my eyes when people would tell me weight loss required a lifestyle change. Now I'm the one saying it: it does. To make it work, you have to make over your mindset. I'm not talking about for 30 days, I'm talking about for all of your days.

That doesn't mean you can't ever have Doritos again. It just means that you're not going to eat them for now. While working toward a goal, it's important to stay focused and on track. Processed foods have a tendency to trigger unhealthy habits. It's best to stay away from most of them while you're getting healthy. Once you've reached your goal and started to maintain, an indulgence periodically isn't going to hurt you, but you'll notice that your desire for the foods of your past is probably not what it used to be.

COUNTING CALORIES

Should you? Shouldn't you? That's something you need to decide for yourself. There's nothing wrong with counting calories or macros. These are tried and true methods that work for a lot of people, but they also require a lot of additional work.

I decided that, for myself, the nutrient content of my food was more important than the calorie content. This wasn't a free pass to eat as much as I wanted; rather, it was an acknowledgement that the type of dieting I did in the past, when I counted calories, didn't work for me. I used to believe that every form of food was permissible as long as it fit into my calorie goals, but all calories are not created equally. I lived on prepackaged meal replacement

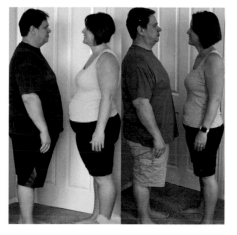

REBECCA AND DAN

We have struggled with weight issues for most of our adult lives. Yo-yo dieting was a way of life for more than 15 years. We would lose weight on the latest fad diet, only to put the weight right back on. Instant Loss got us motivated to learn about the effects of food on the bod! In January 2018 we decided it was time to apply the knowledge we had learned about food and start using Instant Loss recipes. Over the year we have lost a total of 101 pounds together! We have not yet reached our goal weights, so we will continue our journey into this new year and beyond. Brittany and Instant Loss have inspired us and made getting healthy so much more sustainable.

shakes, low-fat freezer dinners, and 100-calorie snack packs. Processed, processed, processed. I was feeding my body, but I wasn't nourishing it, which left me feeling hungry all the time.

Hunger is not a sustainable lifestyle.

I was scared to make any meals or eat anything that didn't fit the set calorie count and it got me thinking, how in the world were humans ever healthy before we started assigning numbers to food? I had to realign my focus. I began putting more effort into finding whole, nutrient-dense, minimally processed foods to fuel myself. I focused on quality and portion size instead of the calorie count. Focusing on quality also meant listening to my body when it spoke to me. I realized what my body was trying to tell me when it gave me hunger pains. It wasn't saying "fill me up," it was saying "fuel me right."

Have you ever eaten an entire 2,000 calories worth of pizza in one sitting and then felt hungry 20 minutes later? I have. It happens because we hear the body say, "I'm hungry," but it's really saying "I need calcium, fiber, potassium, magnesium . . ." The body needs the real stuff. The plant food. The stuff that grows in the soil and comes out of the ground. That stuff.

I replaced counting calories with eating intuitively. Now I listen to my body and feed it when it's hungry.

I don't fear food anymore.

I don't think about the numbers.

This is food freedom!

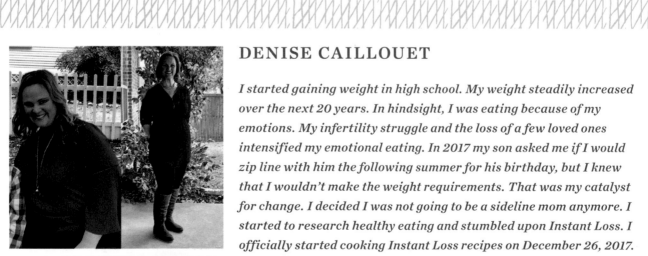

DENISE CAILLOUET

I started gaining weight in high school. My weight steadily increased over the next 20 years. In hindsight, I was eating because of my emotions. My infertility struggle and the loss of a few loved ones intensified my emotional eating. In 2017 my son asked me if I would zip line with him the following summer for his birthday, but I knew that I wouldn't make the weight requirements. That was my catalyst for change. I decided I was not going to be a sideline mom anymore. I started to research healthy eating and stumbled upon Instant Loss. I officially started cooking Instant Loss recipes on December 26, 2017. Since I began using them, I've lost 110 pounds and counting! In June 2018, I was able to ride the zip line with my son for his birthday. We both cried tears of joy and it was truly one of the most special days of my life.

INTUITIVE EATING

Intuitive eating is designed to break our unhealthy diet mentality. It's about honoring your hunger, making peace with food, respecting your fullness, coping with your feelings without using food, and making healthful choices.

DIET MENTALITY	INTUITIVE EATING MENTALITY
What am I allowed to eat?	What do I want to eat?
Will this make me look skinny?	Will this nourish me?
How do I look?	How do I feel?
I exercise so that I can eat.	I eat so that I have energy to exercise.
I am afraid of food.	Food is just food.
I don't like what the scale says, so I am not going to eat today.	I am going to honor my hunger and respect my fullness by eating a nutrient-dense meal regardless of what the scale says.

Eating intuitively coupled with eating real, unprocessed food, freed me from the diet mentality! Everything I was trying to obtain by following food rules I actually obtained by throwing the rules out the window.

The diet industry is a $60-billion-dollar-a-year racket with a 95% failure rate. Your body is not the one that is failing you, it's diet culture. Our pursuit of "health" is prohibiting us from actually experiencing it. We're going about it in all the wrong ways.

Your body knows how to take care of itself. It intuitively knows when we need to rest, move, and eat, but diet culture prohibits you from tapping into your body's knowledge. If you figure it out and truly listen to your body, realizing that you don't need a 30-day plan, a gym membership, a detox tea, a pill, or supplements, then the diet culture loses consumers.

All you need is you. You already possess all the tools you need to be successful.

You have to embrace your body, start listening to it, be mindful of it, and respectful of it. When I began to treat my body like a friend or one of my children, I began to see her in a different light. I began to really love her!

When you take care of your body, it takes care of you. Feed it well and in turn, it will prevent sickness and combat disease. Go for a jog and it will flood you with a rush of endorphins afterward that improve your mood and give you more energy. It's all about listening to your body while integrating the things you already know to be true about the way it functions.

PORTION SIZES

If you're not counting calories, how do you know how much to eat? I use my hands to guide correct food portions for each food group! (Per the Arizona State University School of Nutrition and Health Promotion.)

PROTEIN: It's customary to eat 3 to 4 ounces of a protein source at meal time. A great way to judge how much you should eat is by using the palm of your hand as a portion guide, not including your fingers or thumb.

VEGETABLES: The perfect portion of a side of vegetables at meal time is two hands cupped together, 2 to 4 cups.

FRUIT: A good portion guide for fruit is about one cupped hand, 1 to 2 cups.

HANNA NIBBE

I started cooking with the Instant Loss philosophy and recipes and have lost just shy of 70 pounds in seven months! I was depressed, anxious, and had no energy. Instant Loss showed me a sustainable way to change my lifestyle. I now have energy, my anxiety is at an all-time low, my depression isn't a burden in my life like it used to be, and I have more self-confidence. Thank you, Instant Loss!

STARCHES: Clench your hand to form a fist, that's as much starchy carbohydrates as you should eat for one portion, ½ to 1 cup.

FATS: I'm a fan of healthy fats. It's recommended that a healthy serving of fats like peanut butter, mayo, or oil, is equal to the size of your thumb. However, I'm a bit more indulgent than that and often eat a little more, 1 to 3 tablespoons.

These are practical tips that helped me on my journey. Please do not allow them to overwhelm you. These are tools to use when deciding how to eat, what to eat, and how much to eat. Every person is going to be different. If you find that you need a little more or a little less, that's okay! Respect your hunger and honor your fullness.

INTERMITTENT FASTING AND HUNGER CUES

If you are anything like me, when you hear the word "fasting," you think of starving. But intermittent fasting simply means creating a rhythm for your body. It means fostering a period of time when your body is not digesting, so that during that time, your body can divert that energy to other bodily needs like healing, repair, and breaking down fat stores. Many doctors and dieticians will tell you not to eat after 8 p.m., especially if you are trying to lose weight. They recommend this because when you're sleeping, the body uses that time to regenerate. But if you eat a large meal right before bed, instead of utilizing energy for regeneration, the body uses it to break down all of that food.

In short, I stop eating before 8 p.m. and don't begin eating again until about 9 a.m. This gives my body a 13-hour resting or fasting period. Fasting for a minimum of 12 hours and up to 16 hours is optimal.

While fasting is a great way to help the body function as it should, there's another component which is just as helpful: hunger cues. Being mindful of your hunger cues is very important. Use a hunger scale to help you determine what cues your body is giving you and if it's a good time to eat!

Hunger Scale

1. Angry and Empty
2. Grumpy and Ravenous
3. Irritated and Extra-Hungry
4. Hungry
5. Comfortable

6. Satisfied
7. Completely Satisfied
8. Uncomfortably Full
9. Stuffed
10. Sick

1–3: It should be your priority to never fall into this category. When we let ourselves get over-hungry, we tend to overeat. You can combat this issue by carrying snacks with you wherever you go, being mindful of the time of day, and planning ahead.

4–5: This is the ideal range. When you feel the stirring of hunger pangs or even before you're truly hungry, maybe you're comfortable but you know you're close to being hungry, this is the time to eat. Honor your hunger, and fill your body with nourishing foods.

6–7: Be mindful and choose to eat until you're satisfied. It's okay if you're hungry again in another 2 to 3 hours. The goal shouldn't be to stuff yourself but to be pleasantly content.

8–10: Being stuffed or overfull feels terrible! I like to remind myself when I'm eating a particularly tasty dish that might cause me to overeat that I need to honor my body and respect it when it begins to signal that it's full. Even if there's only a bite or two left on the plate, it's better in the garbage bin or stored as leftovers than sitting like a lump in my belly, making me regret my choice.

Observing your body's natural hunger cues, in conjunction with intermittent fasting, will put your body into a healthy, natural rhythm!

MINDSET

Until you change your thinking, you will always recycle your experiences. Being healthy isn't just about what we put into our bellies, but also what we put into our minds. Finally having the ability to pursue a healthy lifestyle didn't just start with befriending my kitchen, but with changing my mindset about what it meant to be truly healthy.

In the past, I'd spent a lot of time focusing on what I couldn't eat, how it wasn't fair, or how I was dealt a crummy hand in the metabolism lotto. I looked at people who lost weight successfully as an enigma. Sure, I could do it too if I had her motivation, or that person's support system, or someone else's money and resources, or if I liked all those foods. Excuses, deflection, self-pity. I focused on anything to reassure myself it wasn't possible, instead of focusing on how it could be possible.

This required a mental shift that was arguably the most difficult part of my journey. I had to target a quality of life instead of an ideal weight or size, always asking myself, "Does this choice support the life I am trying to create?"

I had to ditch my all-or-nothing mentality. For instance, saying "Oh, I've ruined my healthy eating for today, so I'll just eat junk for the rest of the day" is like saying "Oh, I've dropped my phone, I'll stomp it until it breaks."

I had to acknowledge that I'm not perfect, that I'm going to try my best, and allow that to be enough. I strove for persistence over perfection.

I had to make my goals obtainable. Pursuing an idealistic version of myself and never obtaining it made me feel like a failure. I had to remove the expectations of what I should or shouldn't look like and focus on what was obtainable—being healthy.

I had to pick one thing. Implementing too many major life changes at once was too overwhelming and consistently made me want to quit before I'd even begun. Help yourself be successful by picking one thing at a time and doing that one thing well.

BREAKING THE ADDICTION AND GETTING HELP

I knew that in order to be successful with this life change, I needed to have a safe zone, a place where I could retreat and be safe from temptation. My house became my safe zone. I cleaned out my pantry. Anything that I knew might cause me to falter in my resolve was not allowed in my safe zone, even if that item was a healthy thing. If something was going to trigger my overeating tendency, I tried to steer clear of it. I began to write down in my planner what I ate every day. I kept a water tally and notes to remind myself to take my daily multivitamin.

In the beginning, days were much easier than nights because of the way I'd structured my eating habits. My body was conditioned to eat while we watched TV after putting the kids to bed. Since I was trying to teach my body a different way, there were nights when I had to go to bed early because I couldn't stop obsessing over food. I know now that this was sugar withdrawal. Sometimes drinking water and chewing ice cubes helped, but sometimes it didn't. They say that sugar is ten times more addicting than heroin, and I feel like I truly experienced symptoms of withdrawal.

I had to teach myself the difference between my conditioning and what actual hunger felt like. I'd complain to my husband about how I was starving after having just eaten a snack 30 minutes before. I wasn't really starving, it was just my conditioning. It was the withdrawal.

I had to find a different way to cope with my emotions instead of using food to bury or pacify them. Everything always comes out eventually. If you don't handle your emotions, it's going to manifest itself in other ways. I couldn't figure out how to articulate my feelings or find the vulnerability required to share how broken I was feeling inside. It was easier to say I needed food instead of admitting that I needed help.

Part of this journey for me was finding new ways to manage those big emotions, being more transparent about my feelings with my partner, and finding new ways to handle stress and anxiety. Surprisingly, a lot of my anxiety, exhaustion, and stress began to fade after I altered my diet. I can actually feel a shift in my temperament when I begin to eat poorly now. It makes me feel more anxious, tired, and angry. Y'all, I'm serious—processed food can alter your brain and hormonal chemistry.

I had to learn that I have cravings for a reason and that I need to identify whether they're coming from a place of nutrient deficiency or emotional eating tendencies. Navigating these cravings wasn't always easy, but I accepted that I was going to do all of this perfectly imperfectly and that as long as I'm trying, I'm succeeding.

I now speak what I'm feeling. "I don't really want McDonald's, I'm just feeling overwhelmed and stressed out, and that is how my brain is telling me I can fix it." Then I walk through solutions. Can I calm my anxiety with prayer and breathing exercises? Can I quiet my stress by going for a run or checking a thing or two off of my to-do list?

Finding an ally to talk to is key. Whether that person is a therapist, counselor, girlfriend, or your partner, don't stay silent. Sharing your struggles can be a key way to work through your cravings and realign yourself with your end goal, a healthy lifestyle.

MOTIVATION VS. HABIT

Motivation is fleeting. It comes and goes and cannot be controlled. I realized that I couldn't anchor my success to my motivation, or I would have been done for the first time my husband brought donuts home. So, what did I anchor my success to?

There are so many things we do every day that we don't want to do. Get out of bed, brush our teeth, shower, make breakfast for our kids and get them ready for school and out the door, go to work, pay the bills, clean the house. The list is endless. How is it that we manage to do all of these things every single day without some big motivational push?

Some of these things are habitual, learned habits that become less of a nuisance as we get into a routine and continue to do them over a period of time. They become an almost effortless part of our life, something we don't even think about anymore.

Others may be annoying but a necessity to continue to live the lifestyles we desire. These things don't require motivation either, though it's nice when we have it. Sometimes we have to do things we don't want to, for no other reason than . . . it's good for us—things like paying bills, doing our taxes, and making sure our cars receive proper maintenance. You can see where I'm going with this.

We have to stop thinking about a healthy lifestyle as something that we only do when we're motivated and start thinking about it as one of those things we do because it's good for us, for our families. It's difficult at times, but necessary.

You don't have to be motivated to change. Motivation isn't reliable anyway.

If you can muster the strength to start, I promise you it will begin to turn into a habit—something you won't have to work so hard at anymore because it will become a part of your everyday lifestyle and, over time, will require less thought and energy. So, how do you turn this into a habitual lifestyle change?

It requires hard work, dedication, and choosing to do what's best instead of what is most appealing. It requires denying that voice inside your head, the one that tells you that any form of food could make you feel better or happy. It requires vulnerability, admitting that you have a problem, and reaching out to ask others for help with accountability. It requires doing what's best even when no one is around to witness it.

My Aunt Kim says, "You have to change the wallpaper of your mind before you change your diet. As you begin to love yourself the way you are, you will begin to take care of yourself properly because we take care of the things we love."

THE SOLUTION

Change begins with self-love. You can't hate yourself into health and happiness. I thought my weight was the problem, but it was only a symptom of much deeper issues.

RESPONSIBILITY: I had to acknowledge that I played an active role in getting myself to where I was and that no one could dig me out of the pit but me. By not taking responsibility, I was forfeiting my ability to grow and make lasting changes.

PURPOSE: I had to stop searching for my worthiness in other people and things. I resolved to unfollow anyone on social media who made me feel lesser and focused on finding my passion. I ended up finding a purpose so big that it began to captivate and change all of those around me.

LOVE: I made a promise to myself to begin to prioritize my well-being. To befriend my body, cut out negative self-talk, and love myself the way I love my children. The climb-mountains, brave-stormy-seas kind of love.

Maybe you have a big FAT problem too. Maybe life hasn't gone like you planned, maybe you're struggling with disappointment, battling depression, maybe you're broken.

I've been there and for everything there is a season.

Maybe it's time to move into a new season, one of healing, acceptance, and change.

Take a moment to reflect and ask yourself if there's anything that's prohibiting your ability to grow.

PRACTICALLY SPEAKING

Let's address the pressing question: What can I eat?

I think it's a bit impractical to assume we're going to give up anything for the rest of our lives. I tried restrictive dieting where I cut my diet down to the bare essentials, and you know what? I lost weight! But putting large diet limitations on myself didn't ever last. Overeating is a natural response to restrictive eating. It's a normal response to want exactly what we can't have, and for me, it usually ended in a catastrophic binge fest the second I felt unmotivated, hungry, and tempted.

In 2017, when I decided to pursue health, I decided to give a few things up for a while. It's not that I couldn't have them, I just knew they weren't conducive to healing. Those foods will always be around. The world isn't going to run out of Doritos anytime soon, but I only had two years left in my 20s. I'd already spent all of my teenage years overweight, sick, and limited physically. Did I really want to spend all of my 20s the same the way?

This wasn't a diet. Nothing was ever off limits, but I did begin to cut back on my processed food intake to foster the healthiest life I could. By no means did that mean I was perfect, that I didn't have nights where I enjoyed a piece of Papa John's pizza, or that I didn't have a donut from the shop down the street. But when I did eat takeout, I didn't have the same urge to overindulge anymore because I wasn't restricting it. When I realized I could eat those foods anytime I wanted, keeping portion sizes small to moderate wasn't as much of a struggle.

I stopped beating myself up. I stopped punishing myself with hours of cardio or fasting after I made a choice that I didn't feel stellar about. It was a lifestyle change. When we know better, we do better. It was a learning process.

Now I keep things really simple. If it comes from the earth and is minimally processed, I eat it! I eat all fruits, all vegetables, beans and legumes, meats, healthy fats, and whole grains. I limit processed foods and try to mimic my old favorites by re-creating them with real, whole ingredients.

J.E.R.F. is the motto I live by. It simply means, Just Eat Real Food!

I've been able to refine our diets to best suit our family over the last couple of years. For instance, half of my five do not digest unfermented dairy, red meat, or gluten well, so we limit those things. Those foods are not inherently bad for you—my family just has sensitivities to them.

In this cookbook, you'll find delicious recipes for the entire family that follow the J.E.R.F principal—just eat real food. There is something for everyone whether you're low-carb, keto, sugar-free, vegan, pescatarian, or paleo.

WHAT TO EAT WHEN YOU GO OUT

When I first started this lifestyle change, going out was so intimidating. I didn't know what to eat. Now there's no place we go that I can't find something on the menu or have it modified to suit my tastes. Restaurants are growing more accustomed to accommodating food sensitives and allergies, which is very exciting!

For takeout/fast food, I choose:

* Lettuce wrapped burger. Sometimes called protein style. It's essentially just the meat patty with the vegetables, no bun. If the fast food joint doesn't do lettuce wraps, just ask for bun-less, and they should give it to you like a salad. You can also do this with chicken sandwiches.

* Salads. Most places list the calorie count on the menu now. Choose a low-calorie salad paired with a low-calorie dressing. If ordering half a salad is an option, I usually do that.

* Grilled chicken nuggets

* Fresh fruit

At restaurants, I choose:

* A lean protein like chicken breast or salmon, paired with a vegetable side

* A leafy green salad with a balsamic dressing or vinaigrette

* A lettuce-wrapped burger or chicken sandwich with a side salad or sweet potato fries

* Lettuce-wrapped tacos or tacos with a corn tortilla

* Cauliflower-crust pizza

* A brothy, non–dairy based soup or stew

MELISSA BARTHOLOMEW

I'm in my mid-30s but have had lupus since I was 19, as well as being a kidney transplant recipient in 2010. In the summer of 2017, I found myself the heaviest I'd ever been. I was incredibly stressed as a mom to a wild preschooler, a full-time customer service lead for a large company, and a wife to a soldier who was about to deploy to the Middle East. After my husband left in October, I knew I needed to work on myself in order to keep my health steady in the chaos. It was right around that time I stumbled upon the Instant Loss community on Facebook. The recipes were so simple yet delicious, Brittany was full of good nutrition ideas and tips, plus the support in her group was tremendous. It all helped me find the determination to lose over 25 pounds by April and keep it off, but more importantly I felt fantastic and a lot more comfortable in my own skin. I'm grateful for Brittany and how open she is about her journey with her lifestyle change and the encouragement she gives others. Truly from the bottom of my heart, thank you for sharing your life. I know it's not always easy, but your honesty and genuine nature really do help in so many ways.

WHAT TO EAT AT A GATHERING

I was a bit nervous the first time I went to a family gathering after changing my eating habits. I was doing so well making positive changes, I didn't want to set myself back. To eliminate the fear that there wouldn't be anything there I wanted to eat, I called the hostess and asked her if I could bring a side and a dessert. She happily accepted my offer. Almost every party-giver is happy to accept help in the food department, and that way you know that there are at least two things there you'll want to eat!

This is a lifestyle. It wouldn't be a very practical lifestyle if you were afraid every time you socialized. Here are some practical tips to help:

* Do not avoid social situations. Instead of focusing on the food, focus on the people you're with. Be intentional about living in the moment and enjoying the people around you.

* Eat a small snack or meal before the gathering so that you're not ravenous when you arrive and tempted to overeat. Drink lots of water throughout the evening.

* Do not feel guilty for indulging a little. Enjoy treats in moderation.

* Fill your plate once and do not go back for seconds.

* Do not feel pressured by food pushers, but politely say, "No, thank you." If the person is offended, do not take it personally. The way others feel about your choices is not your problem.

* Do not punish yourself with starvation and hours of cardio. Accept that you are human and not perfect!

* Do not give up on your goals, if you mess up, get right back on track with your next meal.

WHAT TO EAT WHEN YOU'RE BUSY

In recent years, our lives have gotten much more complicated. We always have something to do, somewhere to be, a business call to make, books to write. . . . As our lives evolved, the way we eat evolved too. I have to be more intentional about the way I handle our meals these days.

This is why *Instant Loss: Eat Real, Lose Weight* is going to make your life so much simpler! On page 33, there is a four-week meal plan with meal prepping tips that I hope you utilize.

These are some of my favorite quick and easy recipes, tested by families, so that you can share them with yours!

But, let's face it, sometimes I just don't want to prep. Sometimes, I just want a Sunday afternoon to be about napping and watching reruns of *The Office,* not figuring out what we're going to eat throughout the week. Maybe I should have titled this section *What to Eat When You're Lazy?* Where my lazy girls at? I'm a lazy girl at heart. I can hustle like a boss but at the end of the day, something has got to give and sometimes what gives is meal time.

So, how is this lifestyle change possible when all you want to do is lie on the couch, amidst the piles of laundry, and not move? Here are some of my go-to dinners. They aren't fancy. They aren't overly nutritious. I call them "at least we're not starving" meals. They're essential fallbacks for those nights where making dinner isn't emotionally feasible.

Lightly Salted Rice Cake + Favorite Sandwich Toppings

My kids love rice cakes topped with peanut butter and jelly. Brady and I will do open-faced turkey, chicken, or tuna sandwiches. This literally takes less than 5 minutes to whip up. It's a great fallback dinner on nights when you just can't even.

Serve with a side of carrot sticks, celery, or gluten-free crackers. Arrowhead Mills has a fabulous almond flour cracker.

SHAWNA BEAM

I had my third baby in May 2018, and I had started following Brittany on Instagram while I was pregnant with him. However, I didn't really put any of her recipes into action until about 2 months after he was born. I got a pressure cooker and ordered her book once it released and began eating real food! I started losing the weight pretty fast while breastfeeding (which I was scared to go all-in full force, because I didn't want to lose my milk supply). I had gained way too much with my first pregnancy and could never get it off, and having got pregnant with my third when my second was only 8 months, it definitely wasn't happening then either. But now my youngest is 7 months, and I'm down to my pre-baby weight and feeling great. From my absolute largest (9 months pregnant) I've lost 75 pounds.

Pro-Mom Tip: Once a week, let the kids make dinner! This is an easy dinner to assign them. If your kids are anything like mine, they'll jump at the chance to get "cooking"!

Popcorn and Smoothies

Go out and buy yourself an air popper right now. Don't waste time trying to pop popcorn kernels in your Instant Pot—that's a big ole mess anyway. Grab a $15 air popper at Walmart. That thing will save your life. Now, we're talking survival food, this isn't a lovely steak dinner with kale and cranberry chutney. This is ride or die, kids are crying, and you're about to lose your ever loving . . . you get the picture.

Pop a huge bowl of popcorn, drizzle with butter or coconut oil, and sprinkle with sea salt. Pick a smoothie recipe (page 68) with ingredients that you have on hand, whir that stuff up, and put it in glasses with fancy straws. Then, and this is important part, sit everyone in front of the TV for a nice relaxing family movie night.

My kids think these nights are magical. Really, they're just about mom trying to keep her cool, but hey, everyone wins! We'll eat kale tomorrow. (Or maybe I snuck it in their smoothies . . . I'll never tell!)

Platter of Scrounge

It's late and you're walking from the fridge to the pantry, scrounging back and forth, hoping something premade, delicious, and ready to serve will appear right before your eyes.

On scrounge nights, anything and everything goes. I pull out leftovers, or I take whatever dipping veggies I have in the fridge (carrots, celery, broccoli, cherry tomatoes, cucumber, peppers, etc.) and put them on a platter with some of my homemade ranch (page 262, I always have that stuff ready to go in the fridge for these occasions). I put out any fresh fruit that we have along with deli meat, string cheese, hard boiled eggs, plantain chips, or nuts. It's a snacker's paradise, and everyone just sits around the counter, going to town.

Again, my kids think these nights are magic! They build their own turkey wraps, line celery with peanut butter and raisins, and eat applesauce out of squeeze packets. What's not to love?

ELISSA HUGGINS

The Instant Loss Cookbook *was a game changer. Since starting to use the recipes, my husband and I have lost a combined 65 pounds in 4½ months through diet change and exercise. Even my picky 5-year-old daughter loves the recipes. My pantry has never looked so good!*

The point of this little section is to show you that I'm a regular human mom, just like you! Not every dinner looks as pretty as the photos you see in this book. My family isn't always put together and composed, and I'm most certainly not up for any Suzie Homemaker awards.

With that said, I want you to know . . . you're going to mess up! You're going to have nights where you won't shine and dinner won't turn out. Nights your kids are being kids and you generally just want to go back to bed. That's okay, it means you're normal!

Take a load off. This process is going to be just as messy as everything else in your life, or I don't know, maybe you have it all together, and in that case just skip over this part. Because if you don't have it all together, you might feel like you're failing all the time, and you're already overwhelmed thinking, "How the heck am I going to pull this off?"

I am your kind of people, and I want you to know you are not failing. Pop some popcorn for dinner, build a platter of scrounge, and know that there's probably a million other moms out there doing the exact same thing.

GETTING STARTED

The key to success is to pick something you can stick to. I decided to keep my approach simple. I focused on eating real, minimally processed foods and staying away from anything I had a sneaking suspicion my body might not have been processing well.

I went through my cupboards and refrigerator and began replacing ingredients little by little. For instance, when we ran out of soy sauce, I replaced it with coconut aminos (a gluten-free and soy-free soy sauce replacement). When we ran out of ketchup, I replaced it with a sugar-free organic ketchup. (Primal Kitchen is a great brand.)

I began to keep a food journal with notes about what I ate, how it made me feel, and how the scale correlated. It doesn't need to be an actual journal—I kept notes in my daily planner.

I started drinking water, which is so vital for optimal health, like it was my job. On average you should drink at least 64 ounces of water a day; I personally aim to drink a gallon a day. Our bodies are composed 60% of water, so think of it as a vitamin or nutrient that your body needs in order to thrive. Carrying a water bottle and refilling it throughout the day is a great reminder to get those ounces in!

Making meals at home is key. It's cost-effective, gives you complete control over ingredients, and is empowering. There's something so satisfying about getting in the kitchen and cooking with beautiful ingredients. With these recipes, you'll be able to have the time convenience of a takeout joint in your own kitchen!

You don't have to change overnight. I didn't just wake up one morning reading labels like a pro and making gluten-free bread from scratch. This was a lengthy process that required an open mind and a willingness to welcome change. Start reading, watch a health documentary on Netflix, and become an active participant in your own health. You have so much power over your own well-being, and a lot of it begins with food.

Eat real food, eat appropriate portions, feed your cravings with healthy alternatives instead of denying them, drink water, move your body when you can, and eat what you love. This is about fostering healthy change for our bodies, minds, and spirits.

INGREDIENTS

There may be many ingredients in this book that you are unfamiliar with. As my family began to make over our mindsets concerning food, our pantry also had a makeover. Use this as a guide to better understand why I use the ingredients I use and what substitutions you can make if you have an allergy or don't have a particular ingredient on hand!

Please note that all the recipes in this book were tested with the ingredients listed in the recipe. If you make a substitution that isn't suggested, you may end up with a different result.

EGGS

All of the recipes in this book call for large eggs. I prefer to buy free-range or pasture-raised organic eggs that are certified humane and antibiotic free.

With egg allergies becoming more prevalent, I made sure to test the baked goods in this book with egg substitutes. The two egg substitutes I've found that work the best are:

Flax Egg

MAKES 1 EGG SUBSTITUTE

1 tablespoon flax meal

2 ½ tablespoons water

Add both of the ingredients to small bowl and stir together with a spoon. Let sit for 5 minutes or until the mixture becomes gelatinous and the consistency resembles egg whites.

Aquafaba

Aquafaba is the cooking liquid leftover when you make legumes. Chickpea aquafaba is highly recommended and the only aquafaba used when testing the recipes. It has a slight yellow tinge

EVELIN DITTMAN

Ever since I was little, I was always the bigger child. My mother would point out my flaws. Telling me if clothes were too tight or that my love handles were sticking out. In middle school I thought starving myself was the only way to lose weight. Come high school, I was taking diet pills, skipping meals, and even the most extreme: making myself sick. The weight never came off. I got married and my husband made me feel like a queen. It wasn't until I had kids that I noticed I really needed to do something, so I went back to not eating, until one day I was scrolling through Instagram and saw your transformation pictures. I thought, "Wow, she's beautiful." I clicked on your profile, and little did I know you would save my life. I kept opening your page and reading your stories. And I'd make the recipes you posted. When your cookbook was announced, I swear I was the first one to preorder. I started this journey with heart issues and a weight of 215 pounds, wearing XXL-size clothing. I am currently 100-something (to me, the number doesn't matter anymore) wearing a size medium, and my heart issues are minor. My kids will have their mom for a long time to come, thanks to you.

to it and an egg-white/jelly-like texture. You can use the liquid from canned or home cooked chickpeas. Use 3 tablespoons of aquafaba to substitute 1 large egg.

FATS

Fat has gotten a bad rap throughout the years. Much like carbohydrates, fat is an energy source that the body relies on to function properly. Our cell structure needs healthy fats to thrive! The fats listed below are full of heart-healthy, micronutrients that help keep our cell membranes strong. Healthy fats help boost your nutrient absorption and are essential for healthy living!

I prefer to use organic, minimally processed fats in my cooking: extra-virgin olive oil, avocado oil, and extra-virgin coconut oil. These oils can usually be used interchangeably. When a recipe calls for a specific oil, it's because that is the oil that tastes the best in that recipe.

Butter and Ghee

My family uses two forms of butter, grass-fed salted butter and ghee. Ghee is clarified butter that has been cooked longer to remove all the moisture, caramelizing the milk solids, and providing a rich, nutty taste. My family struggles with a dairy sensitivity, but we all enjoy ghee without any ill side effects. Store-bought ghee can get pricey, so most of the time we make ours at home.

To make clarified butter and ghee, simply cut a stick of butter into pieces and place in a saucepan over medium-low heat. After the butter melts, you will see it bubble and begin to separate. This is the whey separating from the butter. Using a spoon, skim off the whey and put it in your compost bin, or if you're not dairy sensitive, add it to a pan and sauté some spinach in it for a yummy snack!

Cook the butter until it becomes translucent and the milk solids sink to the bottom. This is clarified butter! You can stop here, or continue to cook the butter until the milk solids brown (not burn) and become fragrant. This is ghee!

Let the butter cool for 10 minutes, and then strain it through a cheesecloth into a glass jar. Store at room temperature for up to up to 3 months or in the refrigerator for up to 1 year.

If you have a sensitivity or allergy to dairy, make sure to consult your physician before consuming any dairy product. Coconut shortening is a perfect 1:1 substitute for butter/ghee in the baked goods recipes in this book. If you're making a meat or vegetable dish, substitute one of the oils listed above in the Fats section.

FLOURS

I am a big fan of alternative flours. Most of the traditional wheat here in the U.S. is fortified and enriched with folic acid. Folic acid is the oxidized form of folate. Unfortunately, my family has a difficult time processing it because of a common gene mutation we all share. To learn more, visit instantloss.com/lets-talk-mthfr. For this reason, we use alternative flours in most of our cooking, and all of the recipes in this book are gluten-free. If you do not have a gluten sensitivity, wheat flour is absolutely healthy to consume in modest portions! Just be mindful as wheat can be inflammatory.

Generally, wheat-free flours are tricky to substitute so I highly recommend using the flours suggested in the recipes.

ALMOND FLOUR: Using a blanched, superfine grind of almond flour will yield the best results for baked goods. This flour is best stored in the freezer because it can go rancid quickly. If you have a nut allergy, you can substitute ½ cup cassava flour for every 1 cup almond flour.

GARBANZO BEAN FLOUR: This flour is packed full of protein and relatively low in carbohydrates. It's also inexpensive! If you cannot consume legumes, you can substitute 1¼ cups superfine, blanched almond flour for every 1 cup garbanzo bean flour.

ARROWROOT FLOUR: Arrowroot flour, also known as arrowroot powder and arrowroot starch, helps give baked goods elasticity. It's also a marvelous thickener that can be used in place of cornstarch. If you do not have arrowroot powder on hand, you can substitute tapioca starch or cornstarch 1:1 for arrowroot powder.

COCONUT FLOUR: Super absorbent, a little bit of coconut flour goes a long, long way. If you have a coconut allergy, you can substitute ¼ cup arrowroot powder for every 1 tablespoon coconut flour. Because it's unique, substituting it in large quantities is not recommended, unless you're looking for a science experiment!

BUCKWHEAT FLOUR: Do not let the name fool you, buckwheat flour isn't wheat at all—it's part of the seed family! It's an antioxidant powerhouse that is high in fiber and non-allergenic. Finding it in a traditional grocery store might be tricky, so I typically order mine through Amazon or pick it up at Whole Foods Market.

OAT FLOUR: All oats are gluten-free but not all of them are processed in a gluten-free facility. If you have celiac disease, be mindful and make sure you purchase oats with a gluten-free label to ensure there is no cross contamination. I make my oat flour at home. One cup of oats equals 1 cup oat flour. Use a high-powered blender, like a Vitamix, to grind your oats fresh for an extra boost of nutrient content!

CASSAVA FLOUR: Rich in minerals like calcium, potassium, magnesium, and iron, cassava flour is made from the whole root of the yucca plant and is non-allergenic. This grain-free flour can be a little hard to find though, so I like to order mine through Amazon. If you're not gluten-free, whole wheat flour can be substituted 1:1 for cassava flour.

MASA HARINA: "Dough flour" in Spanish, this is a corn flour treated in lime and water and used to make traditional Mexican dishes. Because of the way masa harina is treated, it makes the corn easier to digest, loosening the hulls away from the kernels and softening the corn. This flour is a great source of iron, calcium, and fiber. Look carefully at the label and try to find a brand that is not fortified or enriched. I use Quaker brand.

PSYLLIUM HUSK POWDER: A fiber made out of the seeds of the plantago ovata herb, psyllium husk powder can help lower blood sugar and lower cholesterol. It also has the added benefit that can aid in weight loss of keeping the body satiated longer! Its ability to help maintain moisture makes it a fabulous addition to baked goods. If you do not have this powder on hand, you can substitute ground flax seed 1:1.

SWEETENERS

MAPLE SYRUP: 100% pure maple syrup is not the same thing as pancake syrup. Pure maple syrup is made from the sap of maple trees. It is then boiled and reduced, getting rid of some of the water content and concentrating the

STELLA DEBIAGGI

I have tried dieting many times, but I'd always give up after a while and gain everything back. But when I heard Brittany say, "Eating should be to feed your body. Always be deliberate about what you put in your mouth," it clicked, and I've been more consistent than I have ever been. Thank you, Brittany, for being so helpful and relatable.

sweetness. Pancake maple syrup is usually made from high-fructose corn syrup or corn syrup and uses artificial flavorings to make it taste more like maple syrup. Pure maple syrup is a pricey ingredient, and it's sometimes tempting to substitute a cheap alternative, but in this case, you really do get what you pay for! Look for pure maple syrup that does not have any added ingredients. If you still can't bite the bullet, you can substitute raw honey 1:1.

COCONUT SUGAR: Also known as palm sugar, this sweetener is made from the sap of flower buds from the coconut palm tree. It's dark, coarse, and a fabulous brown sugar substitute.

AGAVE NECTAR: I use agave sparingly because it really does mimic the traditional response to sugar in the body, but I like it because it's virtually flavorless. Other alternative

ERIN WEINER

I started my health and wellness journey in November 2017. I joined a pretty hardcore gym that offers 30-minute boot camp sessions. While I knew the weight wouldn't fall right off, by February 2018 I was frustrated I had only lost about a pound. Physically I started to feel stronger, but it wasn't enough. That same month I stumbled across Instant Loss on Instagram. I was impressed by Brittany's story and began to dabble in some healthier cooking. By the end of March I had lost nearly 8 pounds. I was still working out as I found my groove and a great group of girls to keep me motivated. Throughout the next few months, I began to cook more and more Instant Loss recipes. My family was on board too (mostly!). I weighed myself mid-June and I was down 20ish pounds. I felt great, and people were noticing. Along the way I would read Brittany's blog posts for motivation—and they were fantastic. I felt like this lifestyle was created for me. I continued to cook whole foods throughout the summer, which is not easy with all the parties, BBQs, and social gatherings. One of Brittany's major pieces of advice that I took away was to bring a dish to pass that you know is "safe" when attending a party or social gathering. I did just that! Fast-forward to today, December 28, 2018 . . . I preordered my cookbook in July and have been using it ever since I received it in October. I'm down nearly 40 pounds and feeling better than ever. I feel as though Brittany has truly helped to jump-start my healthy lifestyle. I have the tools and knowledge to cook something on the fly as needed and also the mental awareness to say no or limit my portion size. I plan to lose another 20 pounds but would be happy with 12 to 15. Thank you, Brittany. I'm not sure I would be in this great place without your motivation, expertise, advice, and recipes!

sweeteners can overwhelm the flavor of a dish, but agave adds just the right amount of sweetness, nothing more. If you do not want to use agave and do not mind possibly altering the recipe's flavor, you can substitute 100% pure maple syrup or raw honey 1:1.

RAW HONEY: Most of the honey that you encounter in the grocery store is made with artificial sugars, like corn syrup, and has little honey, if any, in it. It's always best to find a local source of raw honey. Local honey is a great way to battle season allergies, but if you can't source it locally, any raw, organic honey will do!

MILKS

HEMP MILK: This is my favorite homemade dairy milk substitute! Hemp seeds are a fabulous source of plant protein, and they make a nutrient-packed seed milk that whips up in five minutes! You can find the recipe on page 266.

COCONUT MILK: I use full-fat canned coconut milk in any recipe that calls for milk, and it's a great substitute for heavy cream or half and half. Trader Joe's has a great coconut milk that doesn't contain guar gum. Refrigerated coconut milk typically has a lot of fillers and is mostly water, which is why I prefer to use canned. If you cannot consume coconut milk, cashew milk is a good 1:1 substitute.

KITCHEN TOOLS

My kitchen didn't come together overnight. I've acquired all of these kitchen gadgets and tools over the last ten years as my family's budget permitted. The two things I'd advise that you invest in first are an electric pressure cooker and a high-powered blender, preferably a Vitamix. Investing in your kitchen by having the proper equipment will enable you to work faster and more efficiently, drastically reducing the time you spend inside the kitchen.

Electric pressure cooker

All of the pressure cooker recipes in this book were tested with the 6-quart Instant Pot 7-in-1 Duo. I have serval different electric pressure cookers, and this is by far the brand and model that I love best. If you are using an 8-quart electric pressure cooker, you will need to adjust the recipes according to the manufacturer's specifications, specifically the liquids. This might require you to double some of the recipes.

Air fryer

I stayed off the air fryer band wagon for a long time but at the beginning of 2018, a foodie friend of mine spoke so highly of hers, I knew I had to try it out. OMG, how did I live without one for so long? This gadget is another tool, like the pressure cooker, that makes cooking healthy meals faster and a bit more convenient. The greatest bonus is that is makes food *crispy!*

I love my pressure cooker, don't get me wrong, but you can't cook everything in a pressure cooker, as some things just don't have the right consistency. For this reason, I include recipes using other methods as well.

Don't fret if you don't have an air fryer yet. I include alternate cooking instructions for every air fryer recipe so you don't have to rush out and buy another gadget, although an air fryer will make it faster. All of the air fryer recipes in this book were tested with the PowerXL 5.3-quart Air Fryer, and results with other air fryer brands may vary.

High-powered blender

I hope y'all don't think I'm cheating on my Instant Pot when I say this but . . . if there's one thing I love more than my pressure cooker, it's my Vitamix. And yes, I really do recommend that you get a Vitamix. My in-laws have had their Vitamix for over 20 years—these machines

KYRA STOVALL

I started my Instant Loss journey on January 1, 2018, at 5-feet-9-inches and 352 pounds. I used the free recipes online until March 2018 and then bought the meal plan bundle. I then preordered the cookbook and got it the day after it was released. Through Brittany on Instagram I have stayed motivated and encouraged. Now on Dec 27, 2018, I am 262 pounds and still losing. I've lost 3 pounds this week alone, and that's with Christmas. I can't express the gratitude I have for Brittany and her family.

are built to last. They can do pretty incredible things such as cook food, pulverize grain, and make the smoothest smoothies you've ever had!

Although I have one now, I was unwilling to drop the cash at first. My husband grew up with a Vitamix, so he was all aboard that train, but $300 for a blender? I couldn't wrap my head around it, so we got a Magic Bullet instead. We burned through two Magic Bullets, a Ninja, and a Blendtec in one year! And when I say burned through, I mean I use my blenders so often that I actually burned the motors out! So, we started saving. Our family pitched in one year, and for Brady's birthday, we finally got our Vitamix! That blender has been going nine years strong!

People ask me all the time what I recommend if you can't afford a Vitamix. Honestly, I recommend saving until you can. This is an investment in your kitchen and your family's lives. I get the struggle, believe me, but mark my words, this is a case where you truly get what you pay for. I have the Vitamix 5200, it's an older model. Honestly, you can't go wrong with any model.

Immersion blender

This is a super-budget-friendly kitchen gadget. Typically for $20 to $30, you can get a machine that will make pureeing soups, dressings, and things like mayo, an absolute breeze.

Food processor

You don't need a big ole to-do—I bought a 10-cup model for $40. A food processor makes chopping veggies, grating cheese, and blending things that are hard to dig out of a blender, like doughs and hummus, a breeze! If you can't afford one right now, that's okay. Having a food processor is not a requirement for this book, just something nice to have.

Knives

A good set of sharp knives will save you so much headache. I have carpal tunnel syndrome and chopping veggies with a dull knife is a quick way to induce a flare. Invest in a great set and purchase a sharpener to ensure you're making it as easy on yourself as possible.

Pancake griddle

One of these babies saves me a bundle of time. It allows me to cook so many things at once! I can make all of my burgers at one time, as well as pancakes, English muffin thins, corn tortillas, and a boatload of fried eggs. This was something my mom turned me onto. I'm the oldest of seven kids, so growing up, cooking burritos one at a time on the stovetop wasn't very time-efficient. You can make eight burritos at once on a griddle! I have a 22-inch ceramic griddle I got for about $30.

ELECTRIC PRESSURE COOKER TIPS

Whether you're a seasoned electric pressure cooker user or just a beginner, this is a great recipe book for you! I was so intimidated when my husband brought home our pressure cooker. There were so many buttons, it looked incredibly complicated. Don't feel bad if you didn't unbox yours for a bit—it took me awhile too. I'd encourage you to begin with something simple, like a soup (page 93), or veggie rice (page 239). But really, there's no going wrong with any of the recipes in this book that require an electric pressure cooker! Here are some pro tips that will get you cooking like a seasoned pressure cooker user in no time.

Safety

Use a name-brand pressure cooker that has been through rigorous safety testing and has built-in safety mechanisms. I was terrified of exploding cookers and boiling liquids, which is why my husband chose a pot with ten proven safety mechanisms. Read your instruction manual thoroughly and follow the manufacturer's instructions. I use the Instant Pot 7-in-1 DUO, and in the 5½ years I've owned my pot I've never had a mishap.

Timing

A pressure cooker takes time to build pressure, like an oven takes time to preheat. When you close the lid and program your pot, keep in mind you'll need to wait 5 to 10 minutes for the pot to build pressure before it begins counting down the cook time. To speed up this process, you can preheat your pot using the SAUTÉ function, but this is not required.

Cleaning

After cooking a particularly fragrant dish, your pot can retain the smell even after you wash it. To avoid pot-stink, I do not store my pot sealed. I store the pot and lid separately, or I set

the lid on top of the pot upside down. If there's a particularly stubborn odor, place 2 cups white vinegar inside the pot, seal and lock the lid in place, then hit the steam button. That should clear it right out. Some cooks also choose to purchase a second sealing ring so they have one for sweet and one for savory, but I've never needed to go that far.

Use an abrasive cleaner like Bar Keepers Friend if the stainless-steel pot liner scorches or has difficult-to-remove food stuck to the bottom.

Buttons

The vast majority of buttons on an electric pressure cooker, like the Instant Pot, are pre-sets, and many won't see much use. The ones that I use most often are:

SAUTÉ: This is just like using a pot on the stove. You can use the element underneath the liner of your pressure cooker to preheat the bottom of the pot. This is useful to cook things like vegetables and bacon, and to brown meats to help them retain moisture before you cook them. You can adjust the temperature on this function by pressing the SAUTÉ button additional times. It will cycle through low, normal, and high heat. I cook most everything on normal (medium heat) or high (medium-high heat) depending on the recipe. I specify in the recipe if the default setting is not being used and the temperature needs to be adjusted. Note: If you have an older model, you will have to press the ADJUST button to cycle through the heat settings.

MANUAL OR PRESSURE COOK: This is the button that I use most frequently! Early models of the Instant Pot say MANUAL, but in 2017 Instant Pot changed the name on the button to PRESSURE COOK. It's the same function—it just has a different name. This button gives you the most control. You can choose whether to cook your food at high or low pressure and you can set your custom cook time. To read more Instant Pot tips, visit instantloss.com/ultimate-instant-pot-guide-beginners.

VENT VALVE: The vent valve is the way you seal your pot to pressure cook and release pressure when you're done. When the valve is pushed back into the sealing position, that means the valve is closed and the pot is ready to begin coming to pressure. Recipes in this book will specify when the pressure should be released (by moving the valve into the venting position or letting the pot naturally release the pressure for a period of time before the valve is moved).

The user will know the pot has come to pressure when the silver/red pin at the top of the pot pops up to become flush with the top of the lid. When the pressure has been released, the pin will drop back down inside its chamber, signaling the pot is safe to open.

Always use caution when opening the pot, as the contents are almost always boiling hot.

Cooking Adjustments

In areas with higher altitude, atmospheric pressure is lower. This means that if you live at a higher altitude than me (3,500 feet), you may have to increase the cooking time in some recipes, specifically, the ones with meat. Test one or two of the recipes. If you find that your food has not cooked in the allotted amount of time, you should use the chart below to adjust the cook times in the recipes accordingly.

ALTITUDE	COOK TIME
5,000 feet	+5%
6,000 feet	+10%
7,000 feet	+15%
8,000 feet	+20%
9,000 feet	+25%
10,000 feet	+30%
11,000 feet	+35%
12,000 feet	+40%

MEAL PLANNING

I've found that organizing a meal plan allows me to be more efficient with my time and mindful of what we eat each day. Even if we don't eat exactly what I plan, there is always a week's worth of breakfast, lunch, and dinner ingredients on hand so I am never left wondering what I should make. The vast majority of the recipes in this book use the same ingredients, repurposed in different ways. This ensures that with just a few staple ingredients you'll be able to make several different recipes and it virtually eliminates all food waste.

Below you'll find a four-week meal plan that I hope helps you get organized! You don't have to follow the plan strictly, it's just a guide to show you what several weeks' worth of meals looks like for my family and how I'd prep accordingly.

MEAL PREPPING

I recommend meal prepping on a Sunday so that your meals are easier to prepare throughout the week. Chop vegetables like onions, carrots, and peppers and then store in glass containers in the refrigerator to help cut down on prep time before meals.

If you like freezer meals, pick any of the one-pot meals in the book and place all of the ingredients, except for the liquids, inside a freezer bag. Write the name of the recipe on the bag, along with any additional ingredients you need to add when it's time to cook and the cook time (so you don't have to pull the book out for reference). When you're ready, just empty the bag into your electric pressure cooker, add the liquid, and cook!

I typically do a large prep the first Sunday of the month and prep less the following weeks, so you'll notice there is much more prep the first week with less prep in the weeks that follow.

WEEK 1	DAY 1	DAY 2	DAY 3	DAY 4	DAY 5	DAY 6
BREAKFAST	3 Easy Egg Bites (page 52) Antioxidant Ginger-Berry Smoothie (page 72)	1 Banana Oat Pancake with Whipped Cinnamon Butter (page 64) Tropical Green Smoothie (page 72)	Strawberry-Shortcake Oatmeal (page 55)	Cinnamon-Walnut Breakfast Cake (page 79) Lean Green Smoothie (page 72)	Day 4 breakfast leftovers	3 Easy Egg Bites (page 52) Purple Power Smoothie (page 73)
LUNCH	Curry Chicken Salad (page 157)	Chipotle Chicken Salad (page 160)	Day 1's lunch leftovers	Dill Chicken Salad (page 160)	Honey Ginger Chicken Salad (page 161)	Dump Chicken Salad (page 161)
DINNER	Healthy Hamburger Mac and Cheese (page 171)	Taco Salad with Mexican Crema (page 115)	Loaded Vegetable Beef Stew (page 104)	Coconut Fried Shrimp (page 196) Simple House Salad (page 122)	Grass-Fed Strip Steak over Southwestern Chopped Salad (page 121)	Crispy Orange Cauliflower (page 227) Veggie Brown Rice (page 239)
OPTIONAL SNACK(S)	½ to 1 cup Candied Party Nuts (page 275) OR 1 Cookie Dough Pop (page 313)	1 green apple, cored and quartered with almond butter or tahini	Sliced cucumber with White Bean Hummus (page 283)	Carrot and celery sticks with White Bean Hummus (page 283)	½ to 1 cup Candied Party Nuts (page 275)	1 Cookie Dough Pop (page 313)

Week 1

Sunday Night Prep

Five Days of Chicken Salad for Two (page 156)

Easy Egg Bites (page 52, make and freeze)

Smoothie prep (page 68)

Candied Party Nuts (page 275)

White Bean Hummus (page 283)

Cookie Dough Pops (page 313)

WEEK 2	DAY 1	DAY 2	DAY 3	DAY 4	DAY 5	DAY 6
BREAKFAST	Chia-Berry Banana Pudding (page 49)	The Complete Breakfast Scramble (page 61) Root Juice Smoothie (page 73)	Day 2's leftover breakfast Citrus-Mint Smoothie (page 73)	Pumpkin-Pie Steel-Cut Oats (page 45)	1 Grain-Free Granola Bar (page 287) 3 Easy Egg Bites (page 52)	Pesto-Aioli Tomato Pie (page 58)
LUNCH	Chicken, Wild Rice, and Vegetable Soup (page 106)	Chicken, Wild Rice, and Vegetable Soup (page 106)	Super Sloppy Joe (page 220)	BLT Salad (page 119)	Chicken Bacon Ranch Wrap (page 134)	Lazy Day Minestrone (page 95)
DINNER	Blackened Salmon with Pineapple Avocado Salsa (page 183)	Roasted Eggplant with Pork Ragu (page 205)	Creamy Garlic Chicken Alfredo (page 147)	Tangy Barbecue Beef Back Ribs (page 175) Cauliflower "Potato" Salad (page 253)	The Ultimate Veggie Burger with Basil Pesto Aioli (page 221) on an Amazing Flourless Hamburger Bun (page 89)	Previous day's dinner leftovers
OPTIONAL SNACK(S)	1 Grain-Free Granola Bar (page 287)	1 green apple, cored and quartered with almond butter or tahini	Kale Chips (page 284) OR Cookie Dough Pop (page 313)	Carrot-Mango Smoothie (page 73)	Vegetables of choice with Ranch Dressing (page 262)	1 Grain-free Granola Bar (page 287)

Week 2

Sunday Night Prep

Grain-Free Granola Bars (page 287)

Chia-Berry Banana Pudding (page 49)

Chicken, Wild Rice, and Vegetable Soup (page 106)

Ranch Dressing (page 262)

WEEK 3	DAY 1	DAY 2	DAY 3	DAY 4	DAY 5	DAY 6
BREAKFAST	Bacon, Egg, and Avocado Sandwich (page 63)	Previous day's breakfast leftovers	Strawberry-Shortcake Oatmeal (page 55)	Creamy Spinach and Goat Cheese Frittata (page 43)	Previous day's breakfast leftovers Antioxidant Ginger-Berry Smoothie (page 72)	2 to 4 Super-Seed Chocolate Muffins (page 91) Tropical Green Smoothie (page 72)
LUNCH	Beet and Walnut Salad with Honey Dijon Vinaigrette (page 113)	Roasted Zucchini and Tomatoes with Creamy Garlic Sauce (page 219)	Veggie Spring Rolls (page 224)	Butternut Squash Chipotle Chili (page 235)	Ginger Chicken Stir-Fry (page 150)	Spicy Thai Pizza (page 232) Simple House Salad (page 122)
DINNER	Cowboy Chili (page 167) Golden Sweet Corn Bread (page 80)	Pork Carnitas Tacos (page 210)	Sirloin Steak Strips with Mushrooms and Balsamic Glaze (page 173) Garlic Mashed Cauliflower (page 244)	One-Pot Creamy Chicken Spaghetti (page 131)	Previous day's dinner leftovers	Shredded Chicken Tacos with Homemade Tortillas (page 143)
OPTIONAL SNACK/S	Tortilla Chips with Restaurant-Style Salsa (page 277)	2 to 4 Super-Seed Chocolate Muffins (page 91)	1 green apple, cored and quartered with almond butter or tahini	Lean Green Smoothie (page 72) OR 1 Cookie Dough Pop (page 313)	2 to 4 Super-Seed Chocolate Muffins (page 91)	Previous days' leftovers

Week 3

Sunday Night Prep

Golden Sweet Corn Bread (page 80)
Air Fryer Tortilla Chips with Restaurant-Style Salsa (page 277)

Gluten-Free English Muffin Thins (page 77)
Super-Seed Chocolate Muffins (page 91, make and freeze)

WEEK 4	DAY 1	DAY 2	DAY 3	DAY 4	DAY 5	DAY 6
BREAKFAST	2 Homemade Maple Breakfast Sausages (page 46) 2 eggs, scrambled	1 or 2 Cinnamon Toast Bars (page 51) Purple Power Smoothie (page 73)	Previous day's breakfast leftovers Carrot-Mango Smoothie (page 73)	Banana-Nut Bread Oatmeal (page 57)	Root Juice Smoothie (page 73)	Hearty Biscuits and Sausage Gravy (page 67) Citrus-Mint Smoothie (page 73)
LUNCH	Italian Stuffed Bell Peppers (page 215) Darn Good Green Beans (page 250) Lemon-Garlic Quinoa (page 249)	Broccoli "Cheese" Soup (page 101)	Italian Stuffed Bell Peppers Darn Good Green Beans Lemon-Garlic Quinoa	Mango Mahi-Mahi BBQ Fish Tacos (page 190)	Italian Stuffed Bell Peppers Darn Good Green Beans Lemon-Garlic Quinoa	Leftovers
DINNER	Fish and Chips (page 185)	Simple Chicken Enchilada Bowls (page 139)	Bacon-Wrapped Pork Tenderloin with Fried Apples and Honey Sriracha Glaze (page 208)	Mini Grass-Fed Burgers with Chipotle Mayo (page 168)	Cajun Goulash (page 153)	Autumn Arugula and Sweet Potato Salad (page 125)
OPTIONAL SNACK/S	Spicy Buffalo Almonds (page 276)	1 or 2 Buckeyes (page 308)	1 green apple, cored and quartered with almond butter or tahini	Spicy Buffalo Almonds (page 276)	1 or 2 Buckeyes (page 308)	1 Cookie Dough Pop (page 313)

Week 4

Sunday Night Prep

Lemon-Garlic Quinoa (page 249)

Darn Good Green Beans (page 250)

Italian Stuffed Bell Peppers (page 215)

Spicy Buffalo Almonds (page 276)

Buckeyes (page 308)

Note: Divide the quinoa, green beans, and bell peppers in 4 to 6 equal portions.

Place in the refrigerator to use for lunches throughout the week.

breakfast

Creamy Spinach and Goat Cheese Frittata

Pumpkin-Pie Steel-Cut Oats

Chia-Berry Banana Pudding

Hearty Biscuits and Sausage Gravy

Cinnamon Toast Bars

Easy Egg Bites

Strawberry-Shortcake Oatmeal

Banana-Nut Bread Oatmeal

Pesto-Aioli Tomato Pie

The Complete Breakfast Scramble

Bacon, Egg, and Avocado Sandwiches

Banana Oat Pancakes with Whipped Cinnamon Butter

Homemade Maple Breakfast Sausage

21 Days of Smoothies

CREAMY SPINACH AND GOAT CHEESE FRITTATA

Frittatas are an easy way to get rid of stray leftover veggies! Plus, they keep great in the refrigerator and can be reheated for quick breakfasts throughout the week. This is the core recipe that our family uses for quick breakfasts. I encourage you to use it as a guideline and add your own flair—for example, try adding ground sausage, sweet potatoes, bell peppers, or your own seasoning blend!

SERVES 4 TO 6

8 large eggs

2 tablespoons milk or water

½ teaspoon fine sea salt

¼ teaspoon ground black pepper

1 teaspoon salted butter or ghee, for greasing

½ cup chopped baby spinach

½ cup diced white mushrooms

¼ cup diced tomato

¼ cup crumbled goat cheese

1 cup water

Note: Make the frittata ahead of time and reheat in the microwave for a quick breakfast in the morning. Store in the refrigerator for up to 6 days.

1. Combine the eggs, milk, sea salt, and black pepper in a high-powered blender. Blend on high until frothy, about 30 seconds. You can also whisk the mixture in a large bowl if you do not have a blender.

2. Use butter or ghee to grease a 7-inch baking dish that fits inside your electric pressure cooker. Layer the spinach, mushrooms, tomato, and goat cheese in the bottom of the dish. Pour the egg mixture on top. Cover the pan with foil and place on top of the trivet.

3. Pour 1 cup water into the pressure cooker. Carefully lower the trivet and dish into the pot. Place the lid on the cooker and make sure the vent valve is in the SEALING position. Using the display panel, select the MANUAL/PRESSURE COOK function and HIGH PRESSURE, and use the +/− buttons until the display reads 30 minutes.

4. When the cooker beeps to let you know it's finished, switch the vent valve from the SEALING to the VENTING position, administering a quick release. Use caution while the steam escapes—it's hot. Open the cooker and remove the frittata, then slice and serve warm.

PUMPKIN-PIE STEEL-CUT OATS

My Basic Girl is on full display here . . . I'm a lover of all things pumpkin. As soon as August is over, I go into full fall crazy-girl mode. That means pumpkins on the porch, pumpkin pot-pourri (am I the only one who still uses potpourri?), pumpkins on the brain, and pumpkin in the belly. This delicious autumn-themed breakfast will fulfill all your pumpkin dreams.

SERVES 4

2½ cups water

1 cup gluten-free steel-cut oats

½ cup canned pumpkin puree

¼ cup 100% pure maple syrup

2 tablespoons chia seeds

1 teaspoon pumpkin pie spice

¼ teaspoon fine sea salt

½ cup chopped walnuts or pecans

Almond milk, coconut milk, or Hemp Milk (page 266), for serving (optional)

1. Place the water, oats, pumpkin puree, maple syrup, chia seeds, pumpkin pie spice, and sea salt in an electric pressure cooker and stir to combine.

2. Place the lid on the pot. Make sure the vent valve is in the SEALING position. Using the display panel, select the MANUAL/PRESSURE COOK function and HIGH PRES-SURE, and use the +/− buttons until the display reads 15 minutes.

3. When the cooker beeps to let you know it's finished, switch the vent valve from the SEALING to the VENTING position, administering a quick release. Use caution while the steam escapes—it's hot.

4. Stir in the walnuts and serve with a drizzle of milk of your choice, if desired, to cool the oats faster.

HOMEMADE MAPLE BREAKFAST SAUSAGE

I love to triple or quadruple this recipe. I serve one batch the morning I make the patties and then freeze the rest. On busy mornings I can pull a patty out of the freezer and microwave it for 1 to 2 minutes while I'm scrambling a couple eggs for a quick breakfast or protein-packed snack.

MAKES 8 PATTIES

---

1 pound ground pork

2 teaspoons 100% pure maple syrup

¼ teaspoon dried sage

¼ teaspoon dried thyme

⅛ teaspoon dried rosemary

⅛ teaspoon cayenne pepper

⅛ teaspoon ground nutmeg

½ teaspoon fine sea salt

½ teaspoon ground black pepper

1½ teaspoons extra-virgin olive oil

1. Heat a large cast-iron skillet over medium-high heat.

2. Place the ground pork in a large bowl and gently fold in the maple syrup, sage, thyme, rosemary, cayenne pepper, nutmeg, sea salt, and black pepper with a spoon. Divide the sausage into 8 equal portions.

3. Once the pan has preheated, add the olive oil. Shape the portions into patties between your palms and place in the pan. Cook for 8 minutes on one side, then flip the patties and continue cooking until no longer pink in the middle, about 5 minutes. Serve warm or let cool completely before freezing.

CHIA-BERRY BANANA PUDDING

Simple and quick, this tasty little pudding is a delightful morning treat. Try serving It over a banana to mix things up!

SERVES 2

1 very ripe medium banana, peeled

1 cup fresh or frozen mixed berry blend

½ cup frozen blueberries

2 tablespoons 100% pure maple syrup

1 teaspoon pure vanilla extract

⅛ teaspoon fine sea salt

¼ cup chia seeds

1. Add the banana, berry blend, blueberries, maple syrup, vanilla, and sea salt to a high-powered blender and blend on high until smooth, about 45 seconds. Transfer the mixture to a wide-mouth mason jar and stir in the chia seeds, making sure to work them all the way through the pudding.

2. Refrigerate for 1 to 2 hours or overnight, until the mixture has solidified into a pudding consistency. Serve chilled.

CINNAMON TOAST BARS

In 2018, when I published the *Instant Loss Cookbook*, I released a bundle of recipes to those who pre-ordered the book. People went absolutely crazy over these gooey, addictive breakfast bars, declaring it one of the best recipes I'd ever developed. It would be an injustice to keep it hidden from the world though, so it's finally available for all! These sticky, tasty treats taste like a cinnamon roll and are a breeze to whip up.

——————————— **MAKES 16 BARS** ———————————

Coconut oil cooking spray

2 large eggs

2¼ cups tightly packed superfine blanched almond flour

½ cup raw honey

⅓ cup avocado oil

½ teaspoon baking soda

½ teaspoon fine sea salt

1 tablespoon ground cinnamon

1. Preheat the oven to 350°F. Lightly grease an 8 × 8-inch baking dish with coconut oil cooking spray.

2. In a large bowl, combine the eggs, almond flour, ¼ cup of the honey, the avocado oil, baking soda, and sea salt and stir with a spoon until well combined.

3. In a small bowl, combine the remaining ¼ cup honey and cinnamon.

4. Evenly spread half of the dough across the bottom of the prepared baking dish. Spoon half of the honey mixture over the dough. Evenly spread the remaining dough over the top, then cover with the remaining honey mixture.

5. Bake for 28 to 30 minutes, until the edges have browned and the top is golden. Let cool for 5 to 10 minutes, then cut into 16 bars and serve. Store in an airtight container at room temperature.

EASY EGG BITES

If you have time, making a double batch of these is optimal. Serve some for breakfast and freeze the rest (see Note) for busy mornings. Mix things up and leave out the cheese if you're dairy-free! Try adding broccoli and ham or bacon. This is a great base recipe, so don't be afraid to change it up and get creative.

MAKES 12

1 teaspoon salted butter or ghee, for greasing the pan

9 large eggs

½ cup shredded pepper Jack cheese (optional)

¾ teaspoon garlic powder

¾ teaspoon fine sea salt

¼ teaspoon ground black pepper

1½ cups chopped baby spinach

½ cup diced seeded red bell pepper

1. Preheat the oven to 400°F. Grease a 12-cup muffin pan.

2. Combine the eggs, cheese, garlic powder, sea salt, and black pepper in a high-powered blender. Blend on high until frothy, about 30 seconds. You can also thoroughly whisk the mixture in a large bowl if you do not have a blender.

3. Evenly distribute the spinach and bell pepper among the muffin cups. Pour the egg mixture over the spinach and pepper, filling each cup three-fourths full.

4. Bake for 16 to 18 minutes, until the eggs set up and are cooked through. Transfer to a wire rack and cool for 5 minutes. Run a butter knife around the edge of each cup and pop out the egg bites. Serve warm.

Note: Store the bites in the freezer in an airtight container or freezer zip-top plastic bag for up to 2 months. Reheat in the microwave for 30 to 60 seconds.

STRAWBERRY-SHORTCAKE OATMEAL

Pink and delightful, this breakfast dessert is quite the treat! Don't have fresh strawberries on hand? No need to fret—just blend 1 cup frozen strawberries with 1 cup of the water from the recipe and use instead!

SERVES 4

2½ cups water or milk of choice (use milk with a creamy texture)

1 cup mashed hulled strawberries

1 cup gluten-free old-fashioned rolled oats

2 tablespoons 100% pure maple syrup or agave nectar

1 tablespoon extra-virgin coconut oil

½ teaspoon pure vanilla extract

⅛ teaspoon fine sea salt

¼ cup unsweetened shredded coconut (optional)

1. Place the water, strawberries, oats, maple syrup, coconut oil, vanilla, and sea salt in an electric pressure cooker and stir to combine.

2. Place the lid on the pot. Make sure the vent valve is in the SEALING position. Using the display panel, select the MANUAL/PRESSURE COOK function and HIGH PRESSURE, and use the +/− buttons until the display reads 8 minutes.

3. When the cooker beeps to let you know it's finished, switch the vent valve from the SEALING to the VENTING position, administering a quick release. Use caution while the steam escapes—it's hot.

4. Divide the oatmeal evenly among 4 bowls. Serve warm, topped with shredded coconut if desired.

BANANA-NUT BREAD OATMEAL

This is by far one of my favorite oatmeal recipes ever, buttery and sweet, with a delightful little crunch of nuts.

SERVES 4 TO 6

2 very ripe large bananas, peeled and mashed

2½ cups water

1 cup gluten-free old-fashioned rolled oats

2 tablespoons salted butter or ghee

2 tablespoons 100% pure maple syrup

1 teaspoon pure vanilla extract

⅛ teaspoon fine sea salt

½ cup chopped raw pecans or walnuts

1. Combine the bananas, water, oats, butter, maple syrup, vanilla, and sea salt in an electric pressure cooker and stir to combine.

2. Place the lid on the pot. Make sure the vent valve is in the SEALING position. Using the display panel, select the MANUAL/PRESSURE COOK function and HIGH PRESSURE, and use the +/– buttons until the display reads 8 minutes.

3. When the pot beeps to let you know it's finished, switch the vent valve from the SEALING to the VENTING position, administering a quick release. Use caution while the steam escapes—it's hot.

4. Stir in the pecans and serve warm.

PESTO-AIOLI TOMATO PIE

Packed full of basil and incredible flavor, this pie is reminiscent of an egg-less quiche. It's a great brunch pie as it will easily fit into a breakfast or a lunch spread. It's a bit rich, so a small slice is all you need. Pair it with a fruit or breakfast salad to alleviate some of the heaviness from the crust.

SERVES 4

1 large egg white

½ cup tightly packed superfine blanched almond flour

½ cup arrowroot flour

2 tablespoons salted butter or ghee, plus some for greasing

¼ teaspoon fine sea salt

¾ cup frozen yellow corn kernels, thawed

1 tablespoon chopped fresh basil

1 tablespoon chopped green onion

½ cup Basil Pesto Aioli (page 223)

¼ cup freshly grated Parmesan cheese

½ small heirloom tomato, cut into ¼-inch slices

1. Use butter to grease a 7-inch baking dish that fits inside your 5.3-quart air fryer.

2. Combine the egg white, almond flour, arrowroot flour, butter, and sea salt in a food processor. Process on high until the mixture turns into a crumbly dough or forms a ball, about 15 seconds.

3. Press the dough firmly into the prepared dish, spreading along the bottom and creeping up the sides of the dish, as a pie crust.

4. Scatter the corn kernels on the bottom of the crust, then top the corn with the basil and green onion. In a small bowl, combine the aioli and Parmesan with a fork. Pour the aioli mixture over top, gently spreading it with a spoon to make it even. Cover with the tomato slices, placing them side by side and slightly overlapping. Place the dish inside the air fryer basket and bake at 320°F for 20 to 22 minutes, until the edges lightly brown (see Note).

5. Remove the pie from the air fryer and let cool on a wire rack for 15 minutes before serving.

Note: If you don't have an air fryer, double the recipe and bake the pie in a 9-inch pie pan for 55 minutes in a 350°F conventional oven.

THE COMPLETE BREAKFAST SCRAMBLE

This scramble is special. I think of this as classic American diner food, full of things even your pickiest eater will love.

―――――――――――――――― SERVES 4 ――――――――――――――――

2 cups shredded potatoes

½ cup chopped nitrate-free bacon

5 large eggs

½ cup shredded Colby Jack cheese (optional)

2 tablespoons milk

1 tablespoon salted butter or ghee, plus more for greasing

1½ teaspoons sriracha, plus extra for serving

¼ teaspoon aluminum-free baking powder

2 teaspoons everything bagel seasoning

2 tablespoons chopped fresh chives

1 Roma tomato, cored and diced

½ large ripe avocado, pitted, peeled, and diced

1. Use butter or ghee to grease a 7-inch baking dish that will fit in your 5.3-quart air fryer. Add the shredded potatoes and bacon to the dish and stir to combine.

2. Place the dish inside the basket of the air fryer and bake at 370°F for 10 minutes, stirring once halfway through.

3. Combine the eggs, cheese (if using), milk, butter, sriracha, and baking powder in a blender and puree on high for 30 seconds. Stir in the everything bagel seasoning.

4. Pour the egg mixture over the potatoes and stir to combine. Bake in the air fryer at 370°F for an additional 9 minutes, stirring every 3 minutes (see Note). The eggs should be softly scrambled. They will continue to cook slightly while plating.

5. Stir in the chopped chives and divide the eggs among 4 plates. Garnish with the tomato, avocado, and Sriracha.

Note: If you don't have an air fryer, you can make the scramble on the stovetop. Heat a large cast-iron skillet over medium-high heat. Add 1 tablespoon butter, the shredded potatoes, and bacon and cook, stirring occasionally, until the potatoes are lightly golden, about 7 minutes. Reduce the heat to medium and add the blended egg mixture. Use a spatula to stir the eggs constantly until they are softly scrambled, about 3 minutes. Follow the directions for step 5 above to finish.

BACON, EGG, AND AVOCADO SANDWICHES

I love a good breakfast sandwich, and I really love them when it comes time for meal prep! I'll dedicate a Sunday afternoon once a month to making all different kinds of variants of breakfast sandwiches, wrap them in parchment paper, and freeze. That way we can have a quick, filling breakfast when we're on the go and I don't have to worry about the time crunch. But note that the avocado should be added only when ready to serve instead of prior to freezing.

— SERVES 4 —

¼ cup Homemade Mayo (page 264) or store-bought mayonnaise

2 tablespoons Frank's RedHot sauce

4 Gluten-Free English Muffin Thins (page 77), split in half and toasted

4 large eggs

½ teaspoon fine sea salt

¼ teaspoon ground black pepper

2 tablespoons chopped green onion

1 tablespoon salted butter or ghee

8 nitrate-free bacon slices, cooked

1 ripe medium avocado, pitted, peeled, and sliced

1. In a bowl, stir together the mayo and hot sauce. Spread the mayo mixture over each slice of the toasted muffin thins and set aside.

2. Whisk together the eggs, sea salt, and black pepper in a bowl. Heat a cast-iron skillet over medium-high heat. Add the butter to the pan and let it melt. Then add the egg mixture and green onion butter and cook without stirring for 30 seconds. Once the egg mixture sets on the bottom, gently fold the cooked edges inward and away from the outside of the skillet. You want to form large pieces of egg. Continue to cook, stirring occasionally, until the eggs are softly scrambled, about 1 minute.

3. Divide the scrambled eggs evenly on top of four muffin halves. Place two strips of bacon on each sandwich and top with slices of avocado. Cover with the tops of each muffin thin, cut side down. Serve immediately.

BANANA OAT PANCAKES WITH WHIPPED CINNAMON BUTTER

Not only do these pancakes taste like heaven, they smell like it too! If you do not have a pancake griddle, use a skillet on the stove over medium heat.

--- **MAKES 4 PANCAKES** ---

2 tablespoons salted butter or ghee, at room temperature

2 tablespoons raw honey

½ teaspoon ground cinnamon

2 very ripe small bananas, peeled

2 large eggs

2 cups gluten-free old-fashioned rolled oats

2 tablespoons avocado oil

2 teaspoons aluminum-free baking powder

1 teaspoon pure vanilla extract

¼ teaspoon fine ground sea salt

100% pure maple syrup, for serving (optional)

1. In a small bowl, combine the soft butter, honey, and cinnamon with a fork, mashing the butter into the honey mixture until combined. Whip the mixture for a minute using the same fork or a whisk and set aside.

2. Preheat an electric griddle to 350°F.

3. Combine the bananas, eggs, oats, oil, baking powder, vanilla, and sea salt in a high-powered blender and blend on high for 1 minute.

4. Once the griddle is hot, pour about ½ cup batter for each pancake into the pan. You will yield 4 large pancakes, work in batches if needed. Cook until the bottoms are lightly golden, 1 to 2 minutes. Flip each pancake over with a spatula and cook the other side for 1 minute, until golden on both sides and cooked through. Transfer the pancakes to a plate and keep warm until all are cooked.

5. To serve, spread ½ tablespoon cinnamon butter over each pancake and top with maple syrup, if desired.

HEARTY BISCUITS AND SAUSAGE GRAVY

When I was 16 years old, my family moved to Texas, where biscuits and gravy is a breakfast staple. For me, it was love at first bite. And since my husband, being an Oklahoma boy, loves his breakfasts big and meaty, I knew I needed to find a way to "skinnify" this breakfast classic and make it gluten-free. This might not be how Grandma makes biscuits and gravy, but it's pretty darn close.

SERVES 4

FOR THE BISCUITS

2 large eggs

1 cup gluten-free old-fashioned rolled oats

1 tablespoon Hemp Milk (page 266), or almond milk or other milk of choice

1 tablespoon salted butter or ghee

1 teaspoon aluminum-free baking powder

¼ teaspoon fine sea salt

FOR THE GRAVY

1 pound pork sausage meat

2½ cups Hemp Milk (page 266), or almond milk or other milk of choice

¼ cup buckwheat flour

½ teaspoon fine sea salt

¼ teaspoon ground black pepper

1. Preheat the oven to 425°F. Line a large baking sheet with parchment paper.

2. For the biscuits: In a high-powered blender, combine all the biscuit ingredients and blend on high for 2 minutes.

3. Using a 1½-tablespoon cookie scoop, scoop 8 portions of dough onto the lined baking sheet, arranging them ½ inch apart. Bake for 10 to 12 minutes, until the tops are golden and the bottoms are lightly browned. Remove to a wire rack and let cool.

4. For the gravy: Heat a large cast-iron skillet over medium-high heat. Add the sausage meat and cook, crumbling and stirring with a wooden spoon every couple of minutes, until cooked through.

5. Working quickly, add the milk, buckwheat flour, sea salt, and black pepper to the sausage meat. Whisk to combine and let simmer until the mixture thickens into a gravy, about 30 seconds. Remove from the heat.

6. Serve ¼ cup gravy over each biscuit.

21 days of smoothies

Benjamin Franklin said, "By failing to prepare, you are preparing to fail." Skipping breakfast can lead to overeating at lunch, which can then lead you to skip your afternoon snack, maybe even push back dinner, which leaves you ravenously scouring the cupboards at 10 p.m.

One of the ways that I prepare is by prepping meals ahead of time and storing them in the freezer for busy days to come. Any day, at any time, I can grab a smoothie bag out of the freezer and have it ready in minutes.

Smoothies are a great way to start your day on the right foot! I find that by beginning my day with something light that is full of fruits and vegetables I am more likely to continue eating well the rest of the day!

Assembling smoothie bags for meal prep is incredibly fast and easy! Simply place all of the ingredients, except for the water, inside a freezer-safe bag. As you seal the bag, squeeze as much of the remaining air out as possible before laying it flat inside of your freezer to freeze.

Here's how to stash up to 21 bagged smoothies in your freezer for instant smoothie gratification. When you're ready for a smoothie add water or your favorite milk to your blender, grab a baggie from the freezer, add the contents to your blender, and blend! You can also add these optional add-ins for an extra boost of protein, fiber, and superfood power!

OPTIONAL ADD-INS

* 1 scoop collagen peptides

* 1 scoop plant-based protein powder

* Chia seeds

* Hemp seeds

* Whole golden flax seeds

Voila! Instant breakfast with no kitchen cleanup! My favorite kind of meal.

You can make one or all seven of the smoothies listed below. I like to make three baggies of each one, and have included a grocery list for the ingredients needed for all 21 smoothies. But feel free to pick and choose.

THE SMOOTHIES

* 3 Antioxidant Ginger-Berry Smoothies

* 3 Tropical Green Smoothies

* 3 Lean Green Smoothies

* 3 Purple Power Smoothies

* 3 Root Juice Smoothies

* 3 Citrus-Mint Smoothies

* 3 Carrot-Mango Smoothies

GROCERY LIST

Here is a convenient list to use the next time you go to the store. Simply grab all of these ingredients to have everything you need to make 3 portions of the 7 smoothies listed below.

21 quart-size freezer zip-top plastic bags
Permanent marker
14 ounces baby spinach (6¾ cups)
1 large English cucumber (2¼ cups diced)
1 bunch kale (1½ cups chopped)
1 red cabbage (1½ cups shredded)
2 stalks celery
3 large carrots
1 large fresh ginger root
Fresh mint (2 tablespoons chopped)

Fresh flat-leaf parsley (1 tablespoon chopped)
3 to 4 lemons (⅔ cup juice)
12 mandarin oranges
6 small green apples
3 ripe large bananas
Frozen or steamed beets (3 tablespoons diced)
1 large fresh pineapple or 36 ounces frozen pineapple (4½ cups diced)
36 ounces frozen mango (4½ cups diced)
12 ounces frozen berry blend (1½ cups)
12 ounces frozen blueberries (1½ cups)
Chia seeds (5 tablespoons)
Flax seeds (1½ tablespoons)

ASSEMBLY

Take a moment to read through the ingredients listed for all seven smoothies to make sure you have everything.

To assemble each smoothie three times, work through each recipe one at a time, combining triple the amount of all the ingredients listed (but not the water and ice) and dividing among three quart-size freezer zip-top plastic bags.

Label each bag with the smoothie name and add a note about how much water and ice it requires so you can blend it without having to reference the cookbook again.

lean green
smoothie

citrus-mint
smoothie

carrot-mango
smoothie

purple power
smoothie

tropical green
smoothie

When finished, put all the bags in your freezer. When you're ready for a smoothie add the water that it requires to the blender first, empty a bag into the blender, add any add-on's you desire, ice if needed, and blend on high until smooth.

Note: I wrote the smoothie recipes below in individual servings so that if you'd like to make any smoothie without prepping or freezing first, all you have to do is add all of the ingredients to a blender, liquids first, and blend on high until smooth!

ANTIOXIDANT GINGER-BERRY SMOOTHIE

SERVES 1

1 tablespoon fresh lemon juice

¾ cup frozen berry blend

½ mandarin orange, peeled

1 cup baby spinach

½-inch piece peeled fresh ginger

1½ teaspoons chia seeds

Add ¾ cup water to a blender, add the ingredients above, and blend until smooth.

TROPICAL GREEN SMOOTHIE

SERVES 1

½ mandarin orange, peeled

¼ large ripe banana, peeled

½ cup fresh or frozen diced pineapple

½ cup fresh or frozen diced mango

½ cup baby spinach

¼ cup chopped kale (ribs removed)

¼ cup diced cucumber

1½ teaspoons flax seeds

Add 1 cup water to a blender, add the ingredients above and ½ cup ice (if *not* using frozen fruit), and blend until smooth.

LEAN GREEN SMOOTHIE

SERVES 1

½ to 1 tablespoon fresh lemon juice (depending on how tart you like it)

1 small green apple, cored and quartered

¼ cup baby spinach

¼ cup chopped kale (ribs removed)

¼ cup diced cucumber

¼ stalk celery, diced

¼-inch piece peeled fresh ginger

1 tablespoon chopped fresh flat-leaf parsley

Add 1 cup water to a blender, add the ingredients above, and blend until smooth.

PURPLE POWER SMOOTHIE

SERVES 1

1 teaspoon fresh lemon juice

1 mandarin orange, peeled

½ cup shredded red cabbage

½ cup baby spinach

½ cup frozen blueberries

¼ large ripe banana, peeled

1½ teaspoons chia seeds

Add 1 cup water to a blender, add the ingredients above, and blend until smooth.

ROOT JUICE SMOOTHIE

SERVES 1

1½ teaspoons fresh lemon juice

1 mandarin orange, peeled

½ small green apple, cored

½ cup baby spinach

¼ cup diced cucumber

¼ cup diced peeled carrot

¼ stalk celery, diced

¼-inch piece peeled fresh ginger

1 tablespoon frozen or steamed diced beets

Add 1 cup water to a blender, add the ingredients above and ½ cup ice, and blend until smooth.

CITRUS-MINT SMOOTHIE

SERVES 1

1½ teaspoons fresh lemon juice

1 cup diced fresh or frozen pineapple

¼ small green apple, cored

2 tablespoons chopped mint leaves

Add 1 cup water to a blender, add the ingredients above, and blend until smooth.

CARROT-MANGO SMOOTHIE

SERVES 1

½ large ripe banana, peeled

1 mandarin orange, peeled

1 cup diced frozen mango

1 cup diced peeled carrots

Add 1 cup water to a blender, add the ingredients above, and blend until smooth.

breads, cakes, and muffins

Gluten-Free English Muffin Thins

Cinnamon-Walnut Breakfast Cake

Golden Sweet Corn Bread

Seven-Layer Berry Happy Birthday Cake

Lemon Crumb Bundt Cake

Whole Grain Sandwich Bread

Amazing Flourless Hamburger Buns

Super-Seed Chocolate Muffins

GLUTEN-FREE ENGLISH MUFFIN THINS

We love to start our mornings off with a gluten-free English muffin! They also make great breakfast sandwiches. The easy-peasy muffins take only 10 minutes to make and keep nicely on the counter for a day or two—but last longer in the fridge and also freeze great. So make a bunch now and freeze some for later!

MAKES 8 TO 10 MUFFINS

2 large eggs

⅓ cup unsweetened applesauce

2 tablespoons avocado oil or melted coconut oil

1 tablespoon 100% pure maple syrup

¾ cup gluten-free steel-cut oats

1 tablespoon aluminum-free baking powder

¾ teaspoon baking soda

⅛ teaspoon fine sea salt

Coconut oil cooking spray

Butter, ghee, or coconut oil; Blueberry Jam (page 265); and/or your favorite breakfast sandwich fixings, for serving (optional)

1. In a high-powered blender capable of grinding grain, add the following ingredients in this order: eggs, applesauce, avocado oil, maple syrup, oats, baking powder, baking soda, and sea salt. Blend on high until a batter forms, about 30 seconds.

2. Preheat an electric griddle to 350°F, or a cast-iron skillet over medium-high heat.

3. Lightly spray the heated griddle or skillet with cooking oil spray. Working in batches, use a ¼-cup measuring cup to pour the batter onto the griddle. Cook until little bubbles form on the top of the muffins and the bottoms have browned, about 2 minutes. Using a large, thin spatula, carefully flip each muffin over, doing your best to maintain their shape. Cook for an additional 2 minutes, until the underside has browned and the middle has cooked through. Transfer the muffins to a cooling rack or a large plate. Repeat until all of the batter has been used.

4. Once the muffins have cooled completely, gently slice them in half with a serrated bread knife. Serve topped with butter, jam, or any of your other favorite breakfast fixings. To store, place inside an airtight container or freezer bag and store in the refrigerator for up to 5 days or inside the freezer for up to 4 months.

CINNAMON-WALNUT BREAKFAST CAKE

I love cake for breakfast. This cake is special because it's not only grain-free but it can also be nut-free—if you so choose. This warm, delicious cake keeps well on the counter for several days, so make it on Sunday and have a piece with your coffee throughout the week! A perfect breakfast or dessert.

SERVES 6

4 large eggs

⅓ cup water

½ cup coconut flour

½ cup 100% pure maple syrup

1 teaspoon pure vanilla extract

1 tablespoon ground cinnamon

½ teaspoon fine sea salt

½ teaspoon baking soda

½ cup chopped walnuts

1 teaspoon extra-virgin coconut oil, for greasing the pan

Salted butter or ghee, for serving (optional)

1. Place the eggs, water, coconut flour, baking soda, maple syrup, vanilla, cinnamon, and sea salt in a high-powered blender and blend on high until smooth, about 30 seconds. Stir in ¼ cup of the walnuts with a spoon.

2. Use the coconut oil to grease a 6-cup Bundt pan that fits inside your electric pressure cooker. Sprinkle the remaining ¼ cup walnuts on the bottom on the Bundt pan. Using a rubber spatula, spoon the batter into the Bundt pan and smooth the top.

3. Cover the Bundt pan with foil and place on top of the trivet. Pour 1 cup water into the pressure cooker. Carefully lower the trivet and dish into the pot. Place the lid on the cooker and make sure the vent valve is in the SEALING position. Using the display panel, select the MANUAL/PRESSURE COOK function and HIGH PRESSURE, and use the +/− buttons until the display reads 35 minutes.

4. When the cooker beeps to let you know it's finished, switch the vent valve from the SEALING to the VENTING position, administering a quick release. Use caution while the steam escapes—it's hot.

5. Open the cooker and remove the cake. Remove the foil and let cool for 10 minutes on a wire rack before unmolding onto a plate. If desired, serve with butter or ghee.

GOLDEN SWEET CORN BREAD

This corn bread pairs well with the Cowboy Chili (page 167). Something I really like about baking inside the pressure cooker is that it enables me to make sweets and breads in smaller dishes, so that when we're finished with the meal, the sweets are gone too. If there are leftovers, I'll freeze them in individual portions or put them away so I'm not tempted to snack throughout the evening.

SERVES 8

1 large egg

1¼ cups water

¾ cup masa harina

¼ cup tightly packed superfine blanched almond flour

1 teaspoon aluminum-free baking powder

¼ cup raw honey

2 tablespoons salted butter or ghee, at room temperature, plus some for greasing the pan

½ teaspoon fine sea salt

1. Use a bit of butter to grease a 7-inch baking dish that fits inside your electric pressure cooker (see Note).

2. Add the egg, ¼ cup of the water, masa harina, almond flour, baking powder, honey, butter, and sea salt to a food processor and process on high until a batter forms, about 15 seconds.

3. Using a rubber spatula, spoon the batter into the prepared baking dish. Smooth the top so the batter is even. Cover with foil and place on the trivet.

4. Pour 1 cup water into the pressure cooker and carefully lower the trivet and dish into the pot. Place the lid on the cooker and make sure the vent valve is in the SEALING position. Using the display panel, select the MANUAL/PRESSURE COOK function and HIGH PRESSURE, and use the +/− buttons until the display reads 30 minutes.

5. When the cooker beeps to let you know it's finished, switch the vent valve from the SEALING to the VENTING position, administering a quick release. Use caution while the steam escapes—it's hot.

6. Open the cooker and remove the corn bread. Slice into 8 pieces and serve. To store, place inside an airtight container or freezer bag and store in the refrigerator for up to 5 days or inside the freezer for up to 4 months

Note: Alternatively, the corn bread can be baked, uncovered, in a conventional oven at 425°F for 15 to 20 minutes, until an inserted toothpick comes out clean.

SEVEN-LAYER BERRY HAPPY BIRTHDAY CAKE

With so many allergies amongst our children's friends, it's difficult to find a birthday cake that all kids can enjoy. So I created a gluten-free, nut-free, cane sugar–free, honey-free birthday cake. Can't have eggs? No problem! This recipe also works with an egg replacement, like Flax Eggs (page 229). It comes together quickly and doesn't require you to heat the oven at all! I use a pancake griddle and make two cake layers at a time, but if you don't have a griddle handy, a large cast-iron pan or nonstick skillet will make one layer at a time.

SERVES 10

4 large eggs

1½ cups gluten-free steel-cut oats

⅔ cup sugar-free applesauce

¼ cup 100% pure maple syrup

¼ cup avocado oil

2 tablespoons aluminum-free baking powder

1½ teaspoons baking soda

¼ teaspoon fine sea salt

Avocado or coconut oil cooking spray

6 tablespoons organic berry jam

Coconut Whipped Cream (page 294)

¼ cup sprinkles (optional)

1. Place the eggs, oats, applesauce, maple syrup, avocado oil, baking powder, baking soda, and sea salt in a high-powered blender capable of grinding grain. Blend on high until a smooth batter forms.

2. Preheat an electric griddle to 350°F, or a cast-iron skillet over medium-high heat.

3. Lightly spray the heated griddle or skillet with cooking oil spray. Working in batches, use a ⅓-cup measuring cup to pour the batter on the griddle, you should be able to cook two layers at a time. Use care to ensure that each round is similar in size and shape. These small layers will form your cake. Cook until little bubbles form on the top of each layer and the bottom has browned, about 2 minutes. Using a large thin spatula, carefully flip each layer over, doing your best to maintain its shape. Cook for an additional 2 minutes, until browned on each side and the center is cooked through. Transfer to a cooling rack or large plate. Repeat until you have made seven layers.

4. Once the layers have cooled completely, assemble the cake: Place one layer on a flat surface, like a cake stand, add 1 tablespoon of jam to the top and spread with the back of a spoon to distribute evenly. Top with the next layer and repeat with each of the seven layers, ending with the final layer of cake.

5. Using an offset spatula, frost the cake with the coconut whipped cream, starting with the top, then working your way down the sides until everything is evenly covered. If desired, top with sprinkles. Cut into 10 pieces and serve. Store in the refrigerator and enjoy within 3 days.

LEMON CRUMB BUNDT CAKE

Eating healthy never felt so fancy! This cake will transport you to a fancy coffee shop with your first bite. Be careful about portions though—I know that mega-deliciousness triggers my over-eating tendencies. I make this when we have company coming, or I eat just one portion and freeze the rest for later.

SERVES 10

2 large eggs

1¼ cups tightly packed superfine blanched almond flour

⅓ cup plus ¼ cup coconut sugar

2 tablespoons arrowroot flour

½ teaspoon baking soda

1 tablespoon freshly grated lemon zest

3 tablespoons fresh lemon juice

1 tablespoon avocado oil

½ teaspoon pure vanilla extract

¼ teaspoon almond extract

¼ teaspoon fine sea salt

2 tablespoons salted butter or ghee, plus more for greasing the pan

1. Use butter to grease a 6-cup Bundt pan that will fit inside your 5.3-quart air fryer basket (see Note).

2. In a high-powered blender, combine the eggs, 1 cup of the almond flour, ⅓ cup of the coconut sugar, the arrowroot flour, baking soda, lemon zest and juice, avocado oil, vanilla extract, almond extract, and sea salt. Blend on high for 60 seconds. (Blending ensures the coconut sugar breaks down and combines well with the other ingredients.)

3. In a bowl, combine the remaining ¼ cup almond flour, ¼ cup coconut sugar, and butter. Using a fork, mash the butter into the dry ingredients until the mixture resembles coarse, crumbles the size of beads. Using a spoon, carefully fill the bottom of the prepared Bundt pan with the crumbles, then pour the contents of the blender evenly over the top. Smooth the batter evenly with a spatula. Place inside the 5.3-quart air fryer basket and bake at 310°F for 24 to 26 minutes, until an inserted toothpick comes out clean. Carefully remove the Bundt pan from the air fryer and let cool for 15 minutes.

4. Remove the cake by turning the cake pan over onto a cake stand. Slice into 1½-inch pieces and serve warm. Store covered with plastic wrap at room temperature for up to 3 days.

Note: If you do not have an air fryer, you can bake the cake in a conventional 350°F oven for 30 to 35 minutes.

WHOLE GRAIN SANDWICH BREAD

Brady has aspirations of becoming a pastry chef one day. I blame *The Great British Baking Show*. He can spend days on end in the kitchen, tweaking and altering bread recipes—which is fabulous for me because I don't have the patience for the scientific art of baking. That's why we make such a good match. Through several attempts, Brady finally settled on this simple whole grain bread recipe. It's gluten-free but just as wonderful as "regular" bread. It makes a fabulous sandwich bread, or is a treat to have with a smear of butter alongside a cup of soup.

MAKES 1 SMALL LOAF

2½ cups warm water (about 110°F)

3 tablespoons granulated sugar

2 teaspoons dry active yeast

1 large egg

4 cups gluten-free oat flour

1 tablespoon salted butter, plus some for greasing the pan

1½ teaspoons fine sea salt

1. Grease a standard loaf pan with butter.

2. In a bowl, combine the warm water, sugar, and yeast and let stand for 5 to 10 minutes; the mixture should bubble.

3. Pour the yeast mixture into a stand mixer and add the egg, flour, butter, and salt. Using the flat beater attachment, mix on medium speed for about 60 seconds. The dough mixture will be very wet. Transfer the dough to the loaf pan. Let rise, uncovered, for 1 hour in a warm dry place, until doubled in size.

4. Preheat the oven to 375°F.

5. Bake the bread for 40 minutes, until the top is lightly browned around the edges. Remove from the oven and place on a rack to cool before slicing. Once cool, store in an airtight container or bag at room temperature for up to 3 days.

AMAZING FLOURLESS HAMBURGER BUNS

Sometimes a lettuce-wrapped burger just won't cut it. These tasty gluten-free, nut-free, healthy hamburger buns are a satisfying treat when you just want the bun! They're a must-have with The Ultimate Veggie Burger (page 221).

MAKES 4 BUNS

½ cup ground golden flax seeds

¼ cup psyllium husk powder

1 teaspoon aluminum-free baking powder

½ teaspoon fine sea salt

½ cup tahini (page 267) or store-bought

½ cup warm water

4 large eggs

1 teaspoon raw sesame seeds

1. Preheat the oven to 350°F. Line a small baking sheet with parchment paper.

2. In a small bowl, combine the flax seeds, psyllium husk powder, baking powder, and sea salt. In a medium bowl, whisk together the tahini and warm water.

3. Crack the eggs in a separate bowl and whisk. Add the eggs to the tahini mixture, saving a little bit of egg in the bowl for brushing on the buns later. Combine the tahini and eggs, add the dry ingredients, and mix until everything is smooth. The mixture should form a dough; if it doesn't immediately, wait 15 minutes to allow the flax seeds to absorb the excess moisture.

4. Divide the dough into four balls and place on the lined baking sheet. Wet your hands slightly and shape each dough ball into a 3-inch round. With a pastry brush or your fingers, smear some of the leftover egg over the tops, then sprinkle with the sesame seeds.

5. Bake for 35 to 40 minutes, until the bun tops are golden brown. Remove from the pan and allow to cool completely on a wire rack before slicing. Once cool, store in an airtight container or bag at room temperature for up to 3 days.

SUPER-SEED CHOCOLATE MUFFINS

This just might be the healthiest chocolate muffin you've ever eaten! 100% guilt free, low in sugar, and high in heart-healthy seeds, it's is a great breakfast muffin or something to take on the go when you need a little pick me up! I have a massive 48-cup muffin pan and love to make these in huge batches to stick in the freezer—that way I always have a healthy snack I can stick in my purse on the way out the door. Hemp hearts are hulled hemp seeds—the outside crunchy shell removed. You can find them at your natural grocer or local market.

MAKES 24 MINI MUFFINS

½ teaspoon extra-virgin coconut oil, for greasing the pan

4 large eggs

¼ cup plus 1 tablespoon raw honey

2 teaspoons pure vanilla extract

1 cup gluten-free steel-cut oats

½ teaspoon baking soda

2 tablespoons chia seeds

2 tablespoons whole golden flax seeds

2 tablespoons hemp hearts

¼ cup plus 1 tablespoon cacao powder

¼ teaspoon fine sea salt

1. Preheat the oven to 350°F. Grease a 24-cup mini muffin pan with the coconut oil.

2. In this order, add the eggs, honey, vanilla, oats, baking soda, chia seeds, flax seeds, hemp hearts, cacao powder, and sea salt to a high-powered blender. Blend on high for 45 seconds.

3. Divide the batter among the muffin cups, filling each two-thirds full. Bake the muffins for 9 to 10 minutes, until a toothpick inserted into the middle comes out clean. Let cool on a wire rack for 10 minutes. Remove the muffins from the pan and serve warm. Once cool, store in an airtight container or bag at room temperature for 3 days or in the freezer for up to 4 months.

soups and stews

Lazy Day Minestrone

Potato Leek Soup

Acorn Squash Soup

Broccoli "Cheese" Soup

French Onion Soup

Loaded Vegetable Beef Stew

Chicken, Wild Rice, and Vegetable Soup

LAZY DAY MINESTRONE

Some days I have energy and feel motivated to cook up something spectacular for dinner, but most days I don't. Most days are spent working and running kids around to activities, and by the time we hit 4 p.m., my energy is zapped. Cultivating this healthy eating journey into a long-term lifestyle demanded that I have recipes like this Lazy Day Minestrone in my arsenal. This is a great dump meal.

SERVES 5

---

4 cups frozen mixed vegetables (carrots, broccoli, cauliflower)

3 cups vegetable broth (see page 109)

1 (15-ounce) can diced tomatoes, drained

1 (15-ounce) white beans, rinsed and drained

1 cup gluten-free elbow pasta

1 stalk celery, chopped

5 cloves garlic, minced

1 teaspoon fresh lemon juice

1 teaspoon dried oregano

1 teaspoon dried basil

1 teaspoon extra-virgin olive oil

¼ cup freshly grated Parmesan cheese

½ cup chopped fresh basil

Fine sea salt

Ground black pepper

1. In an electric pressure cooker, combine the mixed vegetables, broth, tomatoes, beans, pasta, celery, garlic, lemon juice, oregano, basil, and olive oil. Stir to combine. Place the lid on the cooker and make sure the vent valve is in the SEALING position. Using the display panel, select the MANUAL/PRESSURE COOK function and HIGH PRESSURE, and use the +/− buttons until the display reads 5 minutes.

2. When the cooker beeps to let you know it's finished, switch the vent valve from the SEALING to the VENTING position, administering a quick release. Use caution while the steam escapes—it's hot. Stir in the Parmesan and fresh basil and season with salt and pepper to taste. Serve warm.

POTATO LEEK SOUP

If you're anything like me, you'll find the name of this soup super intimidating. What the heck is a leek? It's a pretty daunting looking vegetable. Let me put your mind at ease: A leek is just like a massive XL mild green onion, on steroids. That's really, in essence, all leeks are: onion. So if you're not feeling up to tackling leeks yet, don't worry. Substitute a large yellow onion, and you'll wind up with virtually the same soup. Leeks are just a little cooler.

SERVES 6

2 tablespoons extra-virgin olive oil

4 cups chopped leeks (white and light green parts), thoroughly cleaned and chopped

5 cloves garlic, minced

2 pounds red potatoes, peeled and cubed

4 cups chicken broth or stock (see page 108)

2 bay leaves

1 teaspoon dried thyme

1 teaspoon fine sea salt (see Note)

¼ teaspoon ground black pepper

⅓ cup chopped fresh chives, for garnish (optional)

1. Preheat an electric pressure cooker using the SAUTÉ function.

2. When the display panel reads HOT, add the olive oil, leeks, and garlic. Cook, stirring, until the leeks soften, about 5 minutes.

3. Add the potatoes, chicken broth, bay leaves, thyme, sea salt, and black pepper. Place the lid on the pressure cooker and make sure the vent valve is in the SEALING position. Using the display panel, press the CANCEL button. Select the MANUAL/PRESSURE COOK function and HIGH PRESSURE. Use the +/− buttons until the display reads 6 minutes.

4. When the cooker beeps to let you know it's finished, switch the vent valve from the SEALING to the VENTING position, administering a quick release. Use caution while the steam escapes—it's hot.

5. Remove and discard the bay leaves. Use an immersion blender to puree the soup until it's smooth and creamy and there are no chunks left. Garnish with fresh chives, if you like, and serve warm.

Note: If you're using a homemade salt-free stock, you'll need to add ¼ to ½ teaspoon additional sea salt.

Note: This soup freezes great! I like to freeze it in mason jars—just make sure to leave plenty of room at the top for expansion, at least 2 inches. It will last in the freezer for up to 4 months.

ACORN SQUASH SOUP

Looking for a lighter soup to pair with a salad and dessert for a meal with multiple courses? This is your gal. I feel extra fancy when I buy a squash at the store and prepare a soup from scratch. Squash intimidated me for a long time. I didn't grow up eating anything like it. Not only was I unfamiliar with the ingredient, but I didn't know how it was supposed to taste when I did make it. This journey was all about conquering and discovering new things for me—that includes squash!

--- **SERVES 6** ---

1 cup water

1 large acorn squash, halved (see Note)

1 large yellow onion, diced

1 large carrot, peeled and diced

3 cloves garlic, minced

2 tablespoons extra-virgin olive oil

3 cups chicken broth or stock (see page 108)

¼ teaspoon ground nutmeg

¼ teaspoon ground cinnamon

1 teaspoon fine sea salt (see Note)

¼ teaspoon ground black pepper

3 tablespoons dried cranberries (optional)

3 tablespoons salted pumpkin seeds (optional)

3 tablespoons milk of choice (optional)

1. Pour 1 cup water into an electric pressure cooker. Place the trivet inside and set both halves of the squash on top. Place the lid on the pressure cooker and make sure the vent valve is in the SEALING position. Using the display panel, select the MANUAL/PRESSURE COOK function and HIGH PRESSURE, and use the +/− buttons until the display reads 7 minutes.

2. When the cooker beeps to let you know it's finished, switch the vent valve from the SEALING to the VENTING position, administering a quick release. Use caution while the steam escapes—it's hot. Using the display panel, press the CANCEL button to turn off the KEEP WARM function. Open the lid and carefully remove the squash with a pair of tongs. Scrape out the seeds and stringy innards and discard. Remove the flesh from the shell and discard the shell.

3. Rinse and replace the liner of the pressure cooker.

4. Preheat the electric pressure cooker using the SAUTÉ function.

continued on page 100

5. When the display reads HOT, add the onion, carrot, garlic, and olive oil. Cook, stirring, until the vegetables begin to soften, 3 to 5 minutes. Add the squash flesh, chicken broth, nutmeg, cinnamon, sea salt, and pepper, then place the lid on the pressure cooker. Make sure the vent valve is in the SEALING position. Using the display panel, press the CANCEL button. Select the MANUAL/PRESSURE COOK function and HIGH PRESSURE. Use the +/– buttons until the display reads 10.

6. When the cooker beeps to let you know it's finished, switch the vent valve from the SEALING to the VENTING position, administering a quick release. Use caution while the steam escapes—it's hot.

7. Use an immersion blender to puree the soup until it's smooth and creamy and there are no chunks left. Ladle the soup into six bowls and, if desired, garnish each with ½ tablespoon cranberries, ½ tablespoon pumpkin seeds, and a drizzle of milk.

Note: If you're using a homemade salt-free stock, you'll need to add ¼ to ½ teaspoon additional sea salt.

Note: This soup freezes very well! I like to freeze it in mason jars—just make sure to leave plenty of room at the top for expansion, at least 2 inches. It will last in the freezer for up to 4 months.

Note: You can substitute butternut squash if you can't find acorn, these are seasonal items that may be difficult to come by certain times of the year.

BROCCOLI "CHEESE" SOUP

A broccoli cheese soup without the cheese . . . say what? Vegans often use nutritional yeast coupled with a nut or seed to mimic cheese in dairy-free dishes. Now mind you, I don't have it out for cheese or dairy at all. On the contrary, I know that some people thrive on a meat- and dairy-heavy diet. But my family does not, so I've found inventive ways to keep the flavors we love while getting rid of the ingredients that don't agree with us. If you are 100% dairy-free, use avocado oil instead of ghee.

SERVES 5 TO 6

3 cups vegetable stock

1 cup raw sunflower seeds

1 cup Hemp Milk (page 266) or milk of choice

½ cup unfortified nutritional yeast

½ teaspoon turmeric powder

1 teaspoon fine sea salt (see Note)

½ teaspoon ground black pepper

2 tablespoons ghee or avocado oil

2 small carrots, peeled and diced

1 medium red onion, diced

4 cloves garlic, minced

4 cups bite-size broccoli florets

1. Preheat an electric pressure cooker using the SAUTÉ function.

2. Combine the vegetable stock, sunflower seeds, milk, nutritional yeast, turmeric, sea salt, and black pepper in a high-powered blender. Blend on high for 1 minute.

3. When the cooker's display panel reads HOT, add the ghee, let it melt, then add the carrots, onion, and garlic. Cook, stirring often, for 3 minutes. Add the blended sauce and the broccoli and stir to mix everything together.

4. Place the lid on the cooker and make sure the vent valve is in the SEALING position. Using the display panel, press the CANCEL button to turn off the SAUTÉ function, then select the STEAM function and HIGH PRESSURE, and use the +/− buttons until the display reads 1 minute.

5. When the cooker beeps to let you know it's finished, switch the vent valve from the SEALING to the VENTING position, administering a quick release. Use caution when the steam escapes—it's hot. Open the lid, stir the soup, and serve.

Note: If you're using a homemade salt-free stock, you'll need to add ¼ to ½ teaspoon additional sea salt.

FRENCH ONION SOUP

French onion is such a fun, light, brothy soup! It has a delicate flavor that is enhanced when you enjoy it with something. Asiago cheese crisps are a great pairing; or float half of a Gluten-Free English Muffin Thin (page 77) on top of each serving, sprinkle with your favorite cheese, and crisp under the broiler. Heaven!

SERVES 6

4 cups beef broth or stock (see page 108)

3 large white or yellow onions, thinly sliced

3 cloves garlic, minced

2 bay leaves

2 tablespoons salted butter or ghee

1 tablespoon arrowroot flour

2 teaspoons red wine vinegar

2 teaspoons raw honey

1 teaspoon dried thyme

1 teaspoon fine sea salt (see Note)

¼ teaspoon ground black pepper

6 store-bought Asiago cheese crisps (optional)

1. Combine the beef broth, onions, garlic, bay leaves, butter, arrowroot flour, vinegar, honey, thyme, sea salt, and black pepper to an electric pressure cooker. Place the lid on the cooker and make sure the vent valve is in the SEALING position. Using the display panel, select the MANUAL/PRESSURE COOK function and HIGH PRESSURE. Use the +/− buttons until the display reads 10 minutes.

2. When the cooker beeps to let you know it's finished, switch the vent valve from the SEALING to the VENTING position, administering a quick release. Use caution while the steam escapes—it's hot.

3. Remove the lid and press the CANCEL button, then select the SAUTÉ function. Cook, stirring, until the soup thickens a bit, 10 to 15 minutes.

4. Portion the soup into six individual bowls and top with Asiago cheese crisps, if desired. Serve warm.

Note: If you're using a homemade salt-free stock, you'll need to add ¼ to ½ teaspoon additional sea salt.

LOADED VEGETABLE BEEF STEW

Full of vegetables and packed with flavor, this hearty comfort food is sure to become one of your family's favorites.

_____ SERVES 6 _____

1 pound beef stew meat, cut into 1-inch pieces

Fine sea salt

Ground black pepper

2 tablespoons salted butter or ghee

2 cups beef broth or stock (see page 108)

5 large carrots, peeled and cut into 1-inch chunks (see Note)

4 stalks celery, cut into 1-inch lengths

1 pound red potatoes, peeled and cut into 1-inch chunks (2½ cups)

1 large white onion, diced

1 (15-ounce) can diced tomatoes, undrained

1 tablespoon garlic powder

1 tablespoon dried minced onion

1 cup frozen white corn

1 cup frozen peas

1. Preheat an electric pressure cooker using the SAUTÉ function.

2. Liberally season the beef with sea salt and black pepper. When the cooker's display reads HOT, add the butter and let it melt before adding the beef. Cook until the meat is browned on one side, about 2 minutes. Using tongs, flip the beef and let it brown on the other side, about 2 minutes longer.

3. Add the beef broth, carrots, celery, potatoes, white onion, tomatoes, garlic powder, and dried onion. Place the lid on the pressure cooker and make sure the vent valve is in the SEALING position. Using the display panel, press the CANCEL button. Select the MANUAL/PRESSURE COOK function and HIGH PRESSURE. Use the +/− buttons until the display reads 30 minutes.

4. When the cooker beeps to let you know it's finished, let it naturally release the pressure until the display reads LO:15. Switch the vent valve from the SEALING to the VENTING position. Use caution while the steam escapes—it's hot.

5. Stir in the corn and peas; the heat from the stew will thaw and cook them. Serve warm.

Note: If you're using a homemade salt-free stock, you'll need to add ¼ to ½ teaspoon additional sea salt.

Note: If I use organic carrots, I do not peel them as there is a lot of nutrient value in the outside skin. I do wash them well to remove any dirt or debris. When carrots are treated with pesticides, the peel holds the majority of the chemical, so if I use carrots that are not organic, I do peel them. The same goes for potatoes.

CHICKEN, WILD RICE, AND VEGETABLE SOUP

I live in beautiful Southern California, but we're at a higher elevation so we get a little bit of inclement weather during the winter months. I say this with great fear of all of those from Michigan and Canada throwing things at me. I know, we Californians don't really know true inclement weather, but all the same. . .

SERVES 6 TO 8

1 pound boneless, skinless chicken breasts, cut into bite-size pieces

6 stalks celery, diced

1 large sweet potato, peeled and cut into 1-inch cubes

1 large yellow onion, diced

1 yellow squash, diced

4 cups chicken broth or stock (see page 108)

4 carrots, peeled and diced

1½ cups cooked wild rice (see Note)

6 cloves garlic, minced

2 tablespoons dried parsley

1 tablespoon dried thyme

2 teaspoons fine sea salt (see Note)

1 teaspoon ground black pepper

½ teaspoon cayenne pepper

1. Place all ingredients in an electric pressure cooker and stir to combine. Place the lid on the cooker and make sure the vent valve is in the SEALING position. Using the display panel, select the MANUAL/PRESSURE COOK function and HIGH PRESSURE, and use the +/− buttons until the display reads 12 minutes.

2. When the cooker beeps to let you know it's finished, switch the vent valve from the SEALING to the VENTING position, administering a quick release. Use caution while the steam escapes—it's hot. Serve warm.

Note: I love to make this soup when I have leftover rice on hand. It doesn't have to be wild rice, it can be any rice! If you'd like to make wild rice in your electric pressure cooker, combine ½ cup wild rice, 1¼ cups broth or water, and ½ teaspoon fine sea salt in the cooker. Place the lid on the cooker and make sure the vent valve is in the SEALING position. Using the display panel, select the MANUAL/PRESSURE COOK function and HIGH PRESSURE, and use the +/- buttons until the display reads 35 minutes. When the cooker beeps to let you know it's finished, switch the vent valve from the SEALING to the VENTING position and you have 1½ cups rice!

Note: If you're using a homemade salt-free stock, you'll need to add ¼ to ½ teaspoon additional sea salt.

HOMEMADE BONE BROTH

If you haven't made bone broth in your electric pressure cooker yet, you are seriously missing out on one of the best features of your pot. It really is as easy as it sounds: Simply add all of the ingredients to your cooker and let the pot do the rest of the work!

MAKES 4 QUARTS

3 pounds meaty bones of choice (from chicken, beef, lamb, or pork)

4 stalks celery, diced

2 large carrots, diced

1 medium yellow onion, thinly sliced

¼ cup fresh flat-leaf parsley

1 tablespoon apple cider vinegar

1 teaspoon fine sea salt

1. Place 4 quarts of water and all of the ingredients inside your electric pressure cooker. Place the lid on the cooker and make sure the vent valve is in the SEALING position. Using the display panel, select the MANUAL/PRESSURE COOK function, HIGH PRESSURE, and use the +/− buttons until the display reads 90 minutes.

2. When the cooker beeps to let you know it's finished, turn off your pot and let it naturally release the pressure, about 25 minutes.

3. Once the liquid has cooled to warm or room temperature, carefully strain the broth through a fine mesh strainer into a bowl. Ladle the broth into quart-size glass jars and discard the bones and vegetables. Store in the refrigerator for up to 6 days, or freeze in tempered glass jars (with at least 2 inches of space at the top) for up to 6 months.

VEGGIE SCRAP VEGETABLE BROTH

This recipe is a true gem! It costs you very little time and money, but will save you a bundle on buying quality broth at the store. Simply collect the ends of your vegetable scraps, clean them well, and freeze them in an airtight freezer bag until you're ready to make this kitchen staple. If you don't have time to wait while accumulating enough scraps, you can use vegetables of your choice. For the best outcome, I recommend onions, carrots, and celery.

MAKES 4 QUARTS

4 cups vegetable scraps (onion ends, carrot tops, celery ends, bell pepper tops, sweet potato ends, etc.)

5 cloves garlic, crushed

1 dried bay leaf

1 tablespoon dried parsley

1 tablespoon extra-virgin olive oil

1 teaspoon dried rosemary

1 teaspoon dried thyme

½ teaspoon fine sea salt

¼ teaspoon ground black pepper

1. Place 4 quarts of water and all of the ingredients inside your electric pressure cooker. Place the lid on the cooker and make sure the vent valve is in the SEALING position. Using the display panel, select the MANUAL/PRESSURE COOK function, HIGH PRESSURE, and use the +/− buttons until the display reads 40 minutes.

2. When the cooker beeps to let you know it's finished, turn off your pot and let it naturally release the pressure, about 25 minutes.

3. Once the liquid has cooled to warm or room temperature, carefully strain the broth through a fine mesh strainer into a bowl. Ladle the broth into quart-size glass jars and discard the leftover vegetable scraps. Store in the refrigerator for up to 6 days, or freeze in tempered glass jars (with at least 2 inches of space at the top) for up to 6 months.

salads

Beet and Walnut Salad with Honey Dijon Vinaigrette

Taco Salad with Mexican Crema

Buffalo Chicken Salad

BLT Salad

Grass-Fed Strip Steak over Southwestern Chopped Salad

Simple House Salad with Garlic-and-Onion Infused Olive Oil

Autumn Arugula and Sweet Potato Salad

BEET AND WALNUT SALAD WITH HONEY DIJON VINAIGRETTE

Beets have a bit of an earthy flavor and are rich in nutrients like fiber, folate, and vitamin C, so I'm always looking for creative ways to sneak them into our diet. This combination of flavors will have you wondering why beets get such a bad rap—trust me, this is a great simple little salad that offers a bit of reprieve from all the ordinary salads.

SERVES 4 TO 6

1 cup water

8 ounces red beets

10 ounces baby spinach

3 ounces goat cheese, crumbled

½ cup chopped raw walnuts

Honey Dijon Vinaigrette (page 114)

1. Pour 1 cup water into an electric pressure cooker. Place the trivet inside and set the beets on top.

2. Using the display panel, select the MANUAL/PRESSURE COOK function and HIGH PRESSURE, and use the +/− buttons until the display reads 25 minutes.

3. While the beets cook, assemble the salad: Combine the baby spinach, goat cheese, and walnuts in a large bowl and set aside.

4. When the cooker beeps to let you know it's finished, switch the vent valve from the SEALING to the VENTING position, administering a quick release. Use caution while the steam escapes—it's hot. Open the lid and carefully remove the beets with tongs. Place them in a bowl and hold each beet under running water as you slip the skins off. Cut the beets into bite-size pieces, then toss with ¼ cup of the honey Dijon vinaigrette.

5. Keep the beets and the salad separate until serving or the beets will dye everything pink. Divide the salad among four plates, top with the beets, and drizzle with the remaining vinaigrette.

HONEY DIJON VINAIGRETTE

Tangy and sweet, this vinaigrette is a complementary dressing that doesn't overpower the main dish but just highlights all the other flavors.

MAKES ¼ CUP

½ cup avocado oil or extra-virgin olive oil

1 tablespoon Dijon mustard

1 tablespoons apple cider vinegar

1 tablespoon plus 1 teaspoon raw honey

1 tablespoon reduced-sodium Worcestershire sauce

⅛ teaspoon fine sea salt

Combine all ingredients in a wide-mouth mason jar and blend with an immersion blender. Store in an airtight container inside the refrigerator. The dressing will keep for 7 days.

MEXICAN CREMA

This makes a great dressing or taco sauce but it's also phenomenal spread over a rice cake! Top it with fresh tomato, avocado, and cilantro and you have an incredibly tasty snack on your hands!

MAKES 1 CUP

1 cup sour cream or Greek yogurt

½ cup chopped fresh cilantro leaves and stems

1 jalapeño, diced

1 tablespoon fresh lime juice

¼ teaspoon ground cumin

¼ teaspoon fine sea salt

Combine all the ingredients in a wide-mouth mason jar and blend with an immersion blender.

TACO SALAD WITH MEXICAN CREMA

Is anyone else flat-out obsessed with taco salad? It's one of those dishes that is super healthy but feels super naughty. I love taco salad night because I can make each child's bowl individually and tailor it to their personal likes and dislikes. For a really picky kid, just stuff a corn tortilla with all of these yummy fillings and make it taco night!

SERVES 6

2 tablespoons avocado oil

1½ pounds lean ground turkey

1½ tablespoons chili powder

2 teaspoons dried minced onion

1 teaspoon ground cumin

1 teaspoon garlic powder

1 teaspoon fine sea salt

½ teaspoon cayenne pepper

1 cup black beans, rinsed and drained

1 cup canned or frozen white corn kernels, rinsed and drained if using canned

¼ cup pickled jalapeños, drained

5 cups shredded romaine or green leaf lettuce

2 Roma tomatoes, cored and chopped

¼ cup chopped green onions

1 large ripe avocado, pitted, peeled, and diced

4 cups organic tortilla chips (optional)

Mexican Crema (page 114)

1. Preheat an electric pressure cooker using the SAUTÉ function.

2. When the display panel reads HOT, add the avocado oil, ground turkey, chili powder, dried onion, cumin, garlic powder, sea salt, and cayenne. Cook, stirring occasionally, until the turkey browns, crumbles, and is cooked through, 5 to 7 minutes.

3. Add the black beans, corn, and pickled jalapeños to the pot and stir to combine. Switch to KEEP WARM and place the lid on the pot.

4. Assemble the salad by layering the lettuce, tomatoes, green onions, avocado, and tortilla chips (if using) in a serving bowl. When ready to serve, add the turkey mixture, drizzle with the crema, and serve.

BUFFALO CHICKEN SALAD

Tangy and packed full of flavor, this chicken salad is great all by itself—or take all the fixings and roll them up in your favorite tortilla to make buffalo chicken wraps.

—————————————— SERVES 4 TO 6 ——————————————

¼ cup butter or ghee

1 pound boneless skinless chicken breasts

⅓ cup Frank's RedHot sauce

1½ teaspoons red wine vinegar

¼ teaspoon dried minced onion

¼ teaspoon garlic powder

¼ teaspoon fine sea salt

5 ounces arugula

2½ ounces blue cheese, crumbled (optional)

Ranch Dressing (page 262, omit the sea salt)

½ cup shredded peeled carrots

½ cup diced celery

1. Preheat an electric pressure cooker using the SAUTÉ function.

2. Add the butter to the cooker and let melt, evenly coating the bottom of pot. Quickly place the chicken breasts in the pot and add the hot sauce, vinegar, dried onion, garlic powder, and sea salt.

3. Place the lid on the cooker and make sure the vent valve is in the SEALING position. Using the display panel, press the CANCEL button to turn off the SAUTÉ function, then select the MANUAL/PRESSURE COOK function and HIGH PRESSURE. Use the +/− buttons until the display reads 12 minutes.

4. When the cooker beeps to let you know it's finished, let it naturally release the pressure until the display reads LO:25. Switch the vent valve from the SEALING to the VENTING position. Use caution while the steam escapes—it's hot.

5. Carefully shred the chicken using two forks and let marinate in the juices while preparing the salad.

6. Rinse and drain the arugula. If you are using the blue cheese, stir 2 tablespoons into the ranch dressing to make a creamy blue cheese dressing.

7. Assemble individual salads by combining the arugula, carrot, celery, remaining blue cheese if using, and dressing, in individual bowls, then top with the buffalo chicken to serve.

BLT SALAD

On hot summer nights this is a go-to in our household. Even the baby loves it! You can dress it up by adding Best Guacamole Ever (page 269)—or just keep it super simple. Sometimes simple is best.

SERVES 4

FOR THE DRESSING

½ cup Homemade Mayo (page 264) or store-bought mayonnaise

1 tablespoon avocado oil

1 teaspoon reduced-sodium Worcestershire sauce

½ teaspoon organic Dijon mustard

⅛ teaspoon fine sea salt

FOR THE SALAD

1 large head green leaf lettuce, shredded

8 strips nitrate-free bacon, cooked and crumbled

1 cup cherry tomatoes, halved

4 green onions, finely chopped

1. For the dressing: Combine all the ingredients in a small bowl and stir. Set aside.

2. For the salad: Place the lettuce in a large bowl and top with the bacon, tomatoes, and green onions. Toss with the dressing and serve immediately.

GRASS-FED STRIP STEAK OVER SOUTHWESTERN CHOPPED SALAD

Who says you can't enjoy a delicious restaurant-style salad at home? If you are one of those people who only enjoys salad when you go out to eat, and can't seem to find the right balance of ingredients when you're home, give this one a go! It has a fine-dining feel and it cooks up in just 15 minutes.

SERVES 2

FOR THE STRIP STEAK

½ teaspoon dried thyme

½ teaspoon garlic powder

½ teaspoon fine sea salt

½ teaspoon ground black pepper

1 (10-ounce) grass-fed beef strip loin steak

2 tablespoons salted butter or ghee

FOR THE CHOPPED SALAD

1 avocado, pitted, peeled, and diced

2 cups shredded green leaf lettuce

½ cup frozen white corn, thawed

¼ cup diced Roma tomato

¼ cup fresh cilantro leaves, chopped

2 teaspoons fresh squeezed lime juice

¼ teaspoon fine sea salt

⅛ teaspoon ground black pepper

1. For strip steak: Heat a cast-iron skillet over medium-high heat.

2. Combine the thyme, garlic powder, sea salt, and black pepper in a small bowl. Rub half of the spice mixture into one side of the steak, then turn it over and repeat on the backside.

3. Melt the butter in the hot skillet and add the steak. Cook for 3 minutes on the first side, then flip the steak with a pair of tongs and cook for 4 minutes on the other side. This will result in a medium-well steak with a hint of pink inside. For a medium-rare steak cook for 2 minutes on the first side and 3 minutes on the second.

4. Transfer the steak to a plate where it can rest and cool for a few minutes. While the steak is resting, assemble the salad.

5. For the salad: Combine all of the salad ingredients in a large bowl and mix thoroughly to combine. Evenly divide the salad between two plates. Thinly slice the steak into ¼-inch-thick slices and serve on top of the salad.

SIMPLE HOUSE SALAD WITH GARLIC-AND-ONION INFUSED OLIVE OIL

This salad is a game changer. It enables me to eat the food I love without overdoing it. If I know we're going to have something for dinner that might trigger my over-eating tendencies, I whip up a quick house salad, which I enjoy 15 minutes before our meal so I'm not as hungry when it's time to sit down and eat with the family. This is something that I also do when we eat out in restaurants.

This is also a great way to get vegetables into your children. My kids know they don't get any pizza on pizza night until they eat their salad. And let them help! They can build their own salads to their specifications. Getting them involved is a great way to get them motivated to eat healthier. Who doesn't want to try their own kitchen masterpieces?

This salad is great alongside the One-Pot Creamy Chicken Spaghetti (page 131) or the French Onion Soup (page 103).

─────────────────────── SERVES 1 ───────────────────────

1 cup shredded green leaf lettuce

2 tablespoons diced vine-ripened tomato

2 tablespoons diced cucumber

1 tablespoon crumbled feta cheese

2 tablespoons Garlic-and-Onion Infused Olive Oil (recipe follows)

1 teaspoon balsamic vinegar

Fine sea salt

Ground black pepper

Assemble the salad by layering the lettuce, tomato, cucumber, and feta cheese on a plate. Drizzle with the infused oil and balsamic vinegar and top with a sprinkle of sea salt and freshly ground black pepper to taste.

GARLIC-AND-ONION INFUSED OLIVE OIL

MAKES ½ CUP

¼ cup finely chopped
red onion

¼ cup extra-virgin olive oil

1½ teaspoons red wine vinegar

1½ teaspoons dried oregano

1 teaspoon garlic powder

Combine all of the ingredients in a mason jar, screw the lid on tight, and shake vigorously. Use to dress salads with an added drizzle of balsamic vinegar, or use in recipes in place of extra-virgin olive oil. Store at room temperature for up to 3 days.

AUTUMN ARUGULA AND SWEET POTATO SALAD

I am a sucker for a beautiful fall salad, and this one is so pretty. Please take the time to arrange the ingredients in a way that will make you devour them with your eyes before they make their way to your tummy. This is a great platter salad and a show-stopping addition to a Thanksgiving meal.

SERVES 4

2 cups packed arugula

2 cups packed baby spinach

1 large Gala apple, cored and diced

1 cup chopped peeled steamed sweet potato (see Note)

½ cup feta or goat cheese, crumbled

⅓ cup chopped raw walnuts

⅓ cup dried cranberries

¼ cup salted pumpkin seeds

2 tablespoons hemp hearts

¾ cup Raspberry Vinaigrette (page 126)

1. In a large bowl, combine the arugula and baby spinach. Top with the apple, sweet potato, feta cheese, walnuts, cranberries, pumpkin seeds, and hemp hearts.

2. Drizzle with the raspberry vinaigrette and serve.

Note: I like to steam my sweet potatoes in my electric pressure cooker! It's much faster than roasting them. (Although roasted sweet potatoes would make a divine addition to this recipe!) Add 1 cup water to the pressure cooker, place the trivet or a steamer basket inside, and then add small sweet potatoes. Cook for 16 minutes on the MANUAL/PRESSURE COOK function and HIGH PRESSURE, with a quick pressure release when they're finished cooking. My sweet potatoes are usually tiny; I can wrap my hand around them and my fingers will touch. If your potatoes are larger, make sure to add plenty of cook time to compensate, or cut them into quarters.

RASPBERRY VINAIGRETTE

Delightfully pink! This dainty little dressing is not only beautiful in color but also in flavor.

———————————————— **MAKES ¼ CUP** ————————————————

¼ cup red wine vinegar

¼ cup fresh or frozen raspberries

2 tablespoons avocado oil

2 tablespoons 100% pure maple syrup

½ teaspoon dried minced onion

½ teaspoon fine sea salt

Combine all the ingredients in a wide-mouth mason jar and blend on high with an immersion blender. Store in a refrigerator for up to 5 days.

poultry

One-Pot Creamy Chicken Spaghetti

Teriyaki Chicken

Chicken Bacon Ranch Wraps

Garlic Butter Chicken

Simple Chicken Enchilada Bowls

Jerk Chicken with Jicama Slaw

Shredded Chicken Tacos with Homemade Tortillas

Creamy Garlic Chicken Alfredo

Chicken Piccata

Ginger Chicken Stir-Fry

Cajun Goulash

Five Days of Chicken Salad for Two

ONE-POT CREAMY CHICKEN SPAGHETTI

Sometimes a girl just needs some good old-fashioned comfort food. It's a little heartier. I like to serve myself a 1- to 1½-cup portion and pair it with a Simple House Salad (page 122). To ensure that your pasta does not clump together, break it into thirds and layer it crisscross in different directions. This will make it easier to stir when the meal has finished cooking.

SERVES 6 TO 8

1 pound boneless skinless chicken breasts, cut into 1-inch cubes

1 medium red bell pepper, seeded and diced

½ medium yellow onion, diced

1 cup roughly chopped white mushrooms

1 tablespoon extra-virgin olive oil

1½ teaspoons garlic powder

1½ teaspoons fine sea salt (see Note)

½ teaspoon ground black pepper

16 ounces gluten-free spaghetti

3 cups chicken broth or stock (see page 108)

1 cup sour cream (see Note)

1. Preheat an electric pressure cooker using the SAUTÉ function.

2. When the display panel reads HOT, add the chicken, bell pepper, onion, mushrooms, olive oil, garlic powder, sea salt, and black pepper. Using a wooden spoon, stir periodically and cook until the chicken browns on all sides and the onion begins to turn translucent, about 5 minutes.

3. Break the spaghetti into thirds and place in the pot. Cover the pasta with the chicken broth, then place the lid on the pressure cooker. Make sure the vent valve is in the SEALING position. Using the display panel, press the CANCEL button. Select the MANUAL/PRESSURE COOK function and HIGH PRESSURE. Use the +/− buttons until the display reads 6.

4. When the cooker beeps to let you know it's finished, switch the vent valve from the SEALING to the VENTING position, administering a quick release. Use caution while the steam escapes—it's hot.

5. Stir in the sour cream and let sit for 5 minutes before serving.

Note: If you're using a homemade salt-free stock, you'll need to add ¼ to ½ teaspoon additional sea salt.

Note: To make this dairy-free, substitute vegan sour cream, coconut cream, or coconut milk for the sour cream.

TERIYAKI CHICKEN

Basically, I could live off this stuff. There's just something about teriyaki sauce that gets my heart beating faster. Always a hit, this dinner never disappoints and will give even your pickiest eater something to smile about. You might want to double this crowd pleaser.

--- SERVES 4 ---

1 pound boneless skinless chicken breasts

½ cup coconut aminos

¼ cup raw honey

5 cloves garlic, minced

2 tablespoons apple cider vinegar

1 teaspoon grated fresh ginger

¼ teaspoon ground black pepper

1 tablespoon arrowroot flour

6 cups frozen stir-fry vegetables

1 cup fresh or frozen pineapple chunks

Veggie Brown Rice (page 239)

1. Place the chicken breasts, coconut aminos, honey, garlic, apple cider vinegar, ginger, and black pepper inside an electric pressure cooker. Place the lid on the pressure cooker. Make sure the vent valve is in the SEALING position. Using the display panel, select the MANUAL/PRESSURE COOK function and HIGH PRESSURE. Use the +/− buttons until the display reads 15 minutes.

2. When the cooker beeps to let you know it's finished, let it naturally release pressure until the display reads LO:15. Switch the vent valve from the SEALING to the VENTING position. Use caution while the steam escapes—it's hot.

3. Using tongs, remove the chicken from the pot, cut into bite-size pieces, and set aside.

4. Press the CANCEL button and then select the SAUTÉ feature. Add the arrowroot flour to the juices in the cooker and whisk until the teriyaki sauce thickens, about 2 minutes.

5. Add the stir-fry vegetables and pineapple and let them cook in the teriyaki sauce for about 2 minutes. Return the chicken to the pot and serve warm with brown rice.

CHICKEN BACON RANCH WRAPS

Wraps that rival your favorite sub shop? I've got you covered. I'm not kidding, they're that good. Super low in carbohydrates, high in healthy fats and protein, this is a great lunch for keto lovers. Meals like these are great because the heart of the dish is the same, but you can doctor it to suit all of your family's preferences. My kids enjoy a wrap made with a gluten-free tortilla, Brady opts to have his in a pita, and I keep it simple by wrapping the savory chicken mix in butterhead lettuce—or serving it over a salad.

SERVES 6

8 ounces nitrate-free bacon, diced

½ yellow onion, diced

1 pound boneless skinless chicken breasts, cut into 1-inch cubes

½ teaspoon fine sea salt

¼ teaspoon ground black pepper

2 tablespoons salted butter or ghee

2 teaspoons dried parsley

1 teaspoon garlic powder

½ teaspoon dried minced onion

½ cup Ranch Dressing (page 262), plus a couple tablespoons for drizzling

1. Preheat an electric pressure cooker using the SAUTÉ function. After pressing the SAUTÉ button, press the ADJUST button until MORE is highlighted (see Note). When the display panel reads HOT, add the bacon and diced onion to the pot. Cook, stirring, until the bacon is crispy, about 10 minutes. If it begins to stick to the bottom of the pot, add 1 tablespoon of the butter. Use a slotted spoon to transfer the bacon and onion to a paper towel. Leave all those delicious juices in the pot.

2. Season the cubed chicken breasts with the sea salt and black pepper. Add the remaining butter to the pot and then the chicken. Cook, stirring the chicken, until it browns on all sides, about 5 minutes.

3. Add the parsley, garlic powder, and dried onion, then stir. Place the lid on the pressure cooker. Make sure the vent valve is in the SEALING position. Using the display panel, press the CANCEL button. Select the MANUAL/PRESSURE COOK function and HIGH PRESSURE. Use the +/– buttons until the display reads 4 minutes.

continued on page 136

1 head butterhead lettuce, rinsed and separated

1 Roma tomato, cored and diced

2 green onions, chopped

4. When the pot beeps to let you know it's finished cooking, let it naturally release pressure until the display reads LO:10. Switch the vent valve from the SEALING to the VENTING position. Use caution while the steam escapes—it's hot.

5. Using the slotted spoon, transfer the chicken to a separate bowl. Add ½ cup ranch dressing and the bacon/onion mixture to the chicken and combine. Spoon the chicken mixture on the lettuce leaves. Top with the tomatoes, green onions, and a drizzle of ranch dressing, and wrap the leaves around the mixture to serve.

Note: Your pot might not have an ADJUST button; if that is the case just press the SAUTÉ button until MORE is highlighted.

GARLIC BUTTER CHICKEN

This chicken makes a fabulous weeknight dinner! Leftovers are perfect to use throughout the week in salads and soups—and don't forget to save the carcass to make you own homemade chicken broth (see page 108).

— SERVES 6 —

1 (5-pound) free-range organic chicken

1½ teaspoons garlic powder

1 tablespoon fine sea salt

½ teaspoon ground black pepper

2 tablespoons salted butter, melted

½ yellow onion, peeled and quartered

½ Gala apple, cored and quartered

Darn Good Green Beans (page 250)

Garlic Mashed Cauliflower (page 244)

1. Place the chicken in a bowl, remove any giblets (the chicken's organs and/or neck in a small bag) from the cavity and discard. Pat the chicken dry with paper towels. In a small bowl, combine the garlic powder, sea salt, and black pepper. Rub the spice mixture into the chicken skin, making sure to get it inside all of the crevices. Cover with plastic wrap and refrigerate for 4 hours or overnight; if you are in a hurry, you can skip this step.

2. Use a silicone brush to coat the chicken with the melted butter. Fill the cavity three-fourths full with the onion and apple, making sure to leave a space so that the hot air can circulate through the cavity while cooking.

3. Place the chicken inside a 5.3-quart air fryer basket, breast-side down (see Note). Place the basket inside the air fryer housing and bake at 350°F for 70 minutes, carefully turning the bird upside down once halfway through the cook time. Check the temperature: The bird is done when an instant-read thermometer inserted in the fleshy part between a thigh and breast, not touching any bone, registers 165°F.

4. Remove the air fryer basket and let the chicken rest inside for 15 minutes before serving. This allows the juices to drain away from the bird so that the skin remains crispy. Cut the chicken into serving pieces and serve alongside the green beans and mashed cauliflower.

Note: If you do not have an air fryer, you can roast the chicken in a roasting pan in the conventional oven at 450°F for 1 hour and 15 minutes.

SIMPLE CHICKEN ENCHILADA BOWLS

Eating healthy doesn't have to be complicated. In fact, most of the time my family's meals are very simple. Sometimes I'm really good at planning, but most of the time by the end of the day we're all tired, and no one wants to cook. That's when dishes like this come in really handy.

If you have leftover rice or beans in the refrigerator feel free to toss those in the pot too!

SERVES 4

1 pound boneless skinless chicken breasts, cut into 1-inch cubes

2 cups salsa verde

¼ cup cilantro stems and leaves

2 cloves garlic, minced

½ cup sour cream or Greek yogurt (optional)

1 head romaine lettuce, shredded

1 large ripe avocado, pitted, peeled, and diced

2 Roma tomatoes, cored and diced

½ yellow onion, diced

1. Combine the chicken, salsa verde, cilantro stems, and garlic in an electric pressure cooker. Place the lid on the cooker and make sure the vent valve is in the SEALING position. Using the display panel, select the MAUAL/PRESSURE COOK function and HIGH PRESSURE, and use the +/− buttons until the display reads 15 minutes.

2. When the cooker beeps to let you know it's finished, let it naturally release pressure until the display reads LO:12. Switch the vent valve from the SEALING to the VENTING position. Use caution while the steam escapes—it's hot.

3. Stir the sour cream into the chicken mixture, if desired.

4. Divide the lettuce among 4 serving bowls and spoon the chicken on top. Top with the avocado, tomatoes, onion, and garnish with chopped cilantro leaves, if desired.

JERK CHICKEN WITH JICAMA SLAW

Jerk chicken is a Jamaican style of cooking where meat is dry rubbed with a hot spice mixture called jerk spice. For optimum flavor let the seasoned chicken marinate overnight in the fridge.

——————— SERVES 4 ———————

1 pound boneless skinless chicken breasts

1 tablespoon avocado oil

2 teaspoons dried minced onion

1 teaspoon garlic powder

½ teaspoon dried thyme

¼ teaspoon dried parsley

¼ teaspoon allspice

¼ teaspoon paprika

⅛ teaspoon cayenne pepper

⅛ teaspoon red pepper flakes

⅛ teaspoon ground cumin

½ teaspoon fine sea salt

¼ teaspoon ground black pepper

¼ cup chicken broth or stock (see page 108), or water

1½ teaspoons arrowroot flour

Jicama Slaw (page 142)

1. In a large bowl, coat the chicken breasts with the avocado oil. Season with the dried onion, garlic powder, thyme, parsley, allspice, paprika, cayenne pepper, red pepper flakes, cumin, sea salt, and black pepper.

2. Pour the chicken broth into an electric pressure cooker and set the trivet inside. Place the chicken breasts on the trivet and place the lid on the pressure cooker. Make sure the vent valve is in the SEALING position. Using the display panel, select the MANUAL/PRESSURE COOK function and HIGH PRESSURE. Use the +/− buttons until the display reads 16 minutes.

3. When the cooker beeps to let you know it's finished, let it naturally release pressure until the display reads LO:15. Switch the vent valve from the SEALING to the VENTING position. Use caution while the steam escapes—it's hot.

4. Using tongs, remove the chicken from the pot and place on a cutting board. Cut into bite-size pieces.

5. Using tongs, remove the trivet. Press the CANCEL button and then select the SAUTÉ feature. Add the arrowroot flour to the broth in the cooker and whisk until the sauce thickens, about 2 minutes. Return the chicken to the pot and stir. Serve the chicken over the jicama slaw.

JICAMA SLAW

Some might think the star of this dish is the chicken, but really, it's the slaw. Boy oh boy, I could eat this for lunch every day for a week. In fact, I have! The slaw keeps really well in the refrigerator and becomes more flavorful the longer it marinates. Don't get me wrong, the chicken is fantastic, but chicken or no chicken, this slaw can stand alone.

SERVES 4

1 cup julienned peeled jicama (see Note)

¾ cup julienned peeled carrots

¾ cup cored shredded purple cabbage

¾ cup julienned English cucumber

¼ cup thinly sliced red onion

2 tablespoons red wine vinegar

2 tablespoons avocado oil

1 tablespoon fresh lime juice

1 tablespoon chopped fresh cilantro stems and leaves

¼ teaspoon chili powder

⅛ teaspoon cayenne pepper

¼ teaspoon fine sea salt

¼ teaspoon ground black pepper

Combine all of the ingredients in a medium bowl and stir until well combined. Refrigerate until serving, or up to 3 to 5 days.

Note: Some stores carry precut and peeled jicama in the prepared foods section. This is a great way to save yourself some prep time!

SHREDDED CHICKEN TACOS WITH HOMEMADE TORTILLAS

A Taco Tuesday staple in our household, these easy-peasy chicken tacos require almost no preparation. Just dump it all in the pot, shred, and serve in corn tortillas!

SERVES 6

1½ pounds boneless skinless chicken breasts, cut into 1-inch cubes (see Note)

1 cup sugar-free red salsa, plus more for serving

½ cup sugar-free green salsa

¼ cup Taco Seasoning (recipe follows)

12 Three-Ingredient Corn Tortillas (page 281) or store-bought corn tortillas

Best Guacamole Ever (page 269)

1 large head romaine lettuce, shredded

1. In an electric pressure cooker, add the chicken, red salsa, green salsa, and taco seasoning. Try not to let the salsa or taco seasoning touch the bottom of the pot, instead pour it all directly on top of the chicken and do not stir.

2. Place the lid on the cooker and make sure the vent valve is in the SEALING position. Using the display panel, select the MANUAL/PRESSURE COOK function and HIGH PRESSURE, and use the +/– buttons until the display reads 12 minutes.

3. When the cooker beeps to let you know it's finished, switch the vent valve from the SEALING to the VENTING position, administering a quick release. Use caution while the steam escapes—it's hot.

4. Using a hand mixer, carefully shred the chicken inside the pot, draping a kitchen towel over the mixer, your hand, and the pot to ensure the salsa doesn't splatter.

5. Spread the tortillas with guacamole and top with lettuce and the chicken salsa mixture. Serve with additional red salsa.

Note: You can use frozen chicken breasts without cubing them first for this recipe. Just be sure to extend the cooking time to 25 to 30 minutes, depending on the size and thickness of the chicken breasts.

TACO SEASONING

Make your own taco seasoning at home! Store-bought brands can have added sugar, preservatives, and fillers. My homemade seasoning is just as delicious, and cost effective as well.

MAKES ¼ CUP

1½ tablespoons chili powder

2 teaspoons dried minced onion

1 teaspoon garlic powder

1 teaspoon ground cumin

½ teaspoon cayenne pepper

½ teaspoon paprika

1 teaspoon fine sea salt

Place all of the ingredients in a mason jar, screw the lid on tightly, then shake. Label and store inside your spice cabinet.

CREAMY GARLIC CHICKEN ALFREDO

Decadent, creamy, and rich—this delicious alfredo chicken isn't lacking in flavor just because it's dairy-free!

─── **SERVES 6** ───

½ medium yellow onion, diced

1 tablespoon avocado oil

1½ pounds boneless skinless chicken breasts, cut into 1-inch cubes

½ teaspoon fine sea salt

¼ teaspoon ground black pepper

1 pound broccoli florets

½ pound portobello mushrooms, wiped clean and sliced

1 pound gluten-free pasta

FOR THE ALFREDO SAUCE

2 cups water

1 cup raw cashews

2 tablespoons unfortified nutritional yeast

2 cloves garlic, peeled

2 teaspoons fine sea salt

Ground black pepper to taste

1. Preheat an electric pressure cooker using the SAUTÉ function. Add the onion and avocado oil to the pot and cook, stirring, until the onion becomes fragrant and translucent, about 3 minutes. Season the chicken with sea salt and black pepper, add to the pot, and toss with the onion. Cook, stirring, until the chicken is almost cooked through, about 5 minutes. Stir in the broccoli and mushrooms.

2. Place the lid on the cooker and make sure the vent valve is in the SEALING position. Using the display panel, press the CANCEL button. Select the MANUAL/PRESSURE COOK function and HIGH PRESSURE, and use the +/− buttons until the display reads 1 minute.

3. While the chicken is coming up to pressure and cooking, bring a large pot of water to a boil and cook the pasta according to the directions on the package.

4. For the Alfredo Sauce: Place all of the ingredients in a high-powered blender. Blend on high until the sauce begins to steam and becomes thick, about 8 minutes. (If you do not have a high-powered blender, you can blend this in a regular blender and then warm it on the stovetop over medium heat, whisking constantly until it thickens.) Set aside.

5. When the pressure cooker beeps to let you know it's finished, let the pot naturally release pressure until the display panel reads LO:15. Switch the vent valve from the SEALING to the VENTING position. Use caution while the steam escapes—it's hot.

6. Toss the pasta with the sauce and serve the chicken.

CHICKEN PICCATA

Chicken Piccata is an American family dinner classic. It usually consists of battered crispy chicken served in a lemon butter sauce. I lighten it up a bit by keeping it simple and forgoing the breading—you get all the same great flavors in a dish that isn't as calorically dense.

SERVES 4

2 (8-ounce) boneless skinless chicken breasts

½ teaspoon fine sea salt

⅛ teaspoon ground black pepper

2 tablespoons extra-virgin olive oil

½ cup chicken broth or stock (see page 108)

1 tablespoon freshly grated lemon zest

⅓ cup fresh squeezed lemon juice

¼ cup brined capers, rinsed and drained

2 tablespoons salted butter or ghee

2 sprigs fresh thyme

4 to 5 cups arugula (about 3 ounces)

⅓ cup chopped fresh flat-leaf parsley leaves

1. Preheat an electric pressure cooker using the SAUTÉ function.

2. Place the chicken breasts on a cutting board. Butterfly each by placing one hand on the breast and slicing the meat horizontally, cutting all the way through to the other side. Open the breast up and lay flat. Cover with plastic wrap and pound with a meat tenderizer or rolling pin to an even thickness. Lightly sprinkle the chicken with the sea salt and black pepper.

3. When the cooker display reads HOT, add 1 tablespoon of the olive oil to the pot. Add one of the chicken breasts and cook until one side is browned, about 3 minutes. Flip the breast over with tongs and brown the other side, about another 3 minutes. Transfer to a plate. Repeat with the remaining oil and second chicken breast.

4. Add the chicken broth to the pot and scrape up any bits stuck to the bottom. Return the chicken to the pot and add the lemon zest and juice, capers, butter, and thyme.

5. Place the lid on the cooker and make sure the vent valve is in the SEALING position. Using the display panel, press the CANCEL button. Select the MANUAL/PRESSURE COOK function and HIGH PRESSURE, and use the +/− buttons until the display reads 5 minutes.

6. When the pressure cooker beeps to let you know it's finished, let the pot naturally release pressure until the display panel reads LO:15. Switch the vent valve from the SEALING to the VENTING position. Use caution while the steam escapes—it's hot.

7. Serve each chicken breast over a bed of arugula, drizzle the pan sauce over the tops, and sprinkle with fresh parsley.

GINGER CHICKEN STIR-FRY

Here's one of the easiest and most popular ways I get dinner on the table: Stir-fry tender chicken with crisp vegetables and a lovely ginger sauce. Don't be afraid to swap out the veggies listed for whatever you have on hand. It's a great dish to use up some of those odds and ends in the back of the refrigerator!

SERVES 2

1 (8-ounce) boneless skinless chicken breast, sliced into ¼-inch strips

¼ teaspoon fine sea salt

⅛ teaspoon ground black pepper

2 tablespoons extra-virgin olive oil

1½ cups broccoli florets, cut into small pieces

2 mini sweet bell peppers, seeded and diced

2 white mushrooms, thinly sliced

4 cloves garlic, minced

1 teaspoon grated fresh ginger

2 teaspoons coconut aminos

1 cup riced cauliflower

2 green onions, finely chopped

1. Heat a large cast-iron skillet over medium-high heat.

2. Sprinkle the chicken with the sea salt and black pepper. Once the pan has heated, add the olive oil and chicken and cook, stirring, until the chicken is nearly cooked through, about 3 minutes.

3. Add the broccoli, bell peppers, mushrooms, garlic, ginger, and coconut aminos and cook, stirring, until the broccoli is tender and everything is cooked through. Add the cauliflower rice, mix everything together, and continue to cook, stirring, for 1 minute.

4. Remove from the heat, sprinkle with the green onions, and serve.

CAJUN GOULASH

This is one of the most loved recipes on my website, InstantLoss.com. Hailed as excellent, easy, and delicious, it's earned its spot here in this book!

——————— SERVES 6 ———————

2 tablespoons salted butter or ghee

1 red bell pepper, seeded and thinly sliced

1 green bell pepper, seeded and thinly sliced

1 yellow onion, thinly sliced

½ teaspoon fine sea salt (see Note)

¼ teaspoon ground black pepper

1 pound 10 ounces ground turkey

3 cloves garlic, minced

4 Roma tomatoes, cored and diced

2 cups chicken broth or stock (see page 108)

1 cup full-fat canned coconut milk

8 ounces gluten-free elbow pasta

5 teaspoons Cajun Seasoning (recipe follows)

⅛ teaspoon cayenne pepper

½ cup finely chopped green onions

1. Preheat an electric pressure cooker using the SAUTÉ function.

2. When the display panel reads HOT, add the butter, bell peppers, and onion and season with the sea salt and black pepper. Cook, stirring, for 3 minutes. Add the ground turkey and garlic and cook, stirring, until the turkey has cooked through and the vegetables have softened, about 5 minutes.

3. Layer in the next ingredients in the order listed: tomatoes, chicken broth, coconut milk, pasta, and Cajun seasoning.

4. Place the lid on the cooker and make sure the vent valve is in the SEALING position. Using the display panel, press the CANCEL button to turn off the SAUTÉ function, then select the MANUAL/PRESSURE COOK function and HIGH PRESSURE. Use the +/− buttons until the display reads 4 minutes.

5. When the cooker beeps to let you know it's finished, switch the vent valve from the SEALING to the VENTING position, administering a quick release. Use caution while the steam escapes—it's hot.

6. Let the goulash sit for about 10 minutes to thicken. Stir to combine, top with the cayenne pepper and green onions, and serve.

Note: If you're using a homemade salt-free stock, you'll need to add ¼ to ½ teaspoon additional sea salt.

CAJUN SEASONING

MAKES ½ CUP

4 teaspoons fine sea salt

4 teaspoons garlic powder

4 teaspoons paprika

2½ teaspoons dried oregano

2½ teaspoons dried thyme

2 teaspoons ground black pepper

2 teaspoons onion powder

2 teaspoons cayenne pepper

1 teaspoon red pepper flakes

Combine all the ingredients in a mason jar, screw the lid on tightly, then shake. Label and store in your spice cabinet.

five days of chicken salad for two

Do not let yourself fall into the busy trap. It is important that you make time to eat! Oftentimes I can get going and blow through the day, fueled by eating my kid's leftovers instead of creating a delicious nutrient-dense meal for myself that would keep me full until snack or dinner time.

My health, my happiness, and what I'm eating is important and it is a priority to me. On weeks that I know I'll be too busy to cook, I set a bit of time aside on Sunday to prepare quick grab-and-go meals to enjoy throughout the week—no matter how little time I have.

This is a meal plan for five days of chicken salad for two. Each day has a new salad that you can enjoy over a bed of greens, on top of a lightly salted rice cake, or inside a low-carb tortilla. I recommend reading through the directions before you begin cooking, although most of the ingredients will be things you already have on hand and there is little prep required.

FOR THE CHICKEN

* 2 pounds boneless skinless chicken breasts, fresh or frozen

* 1 teaspoon fine sea salt

* ¼ teaspoon ground black pepper

* 1 cup water

FOR THE SALADS

1 cup Homemade Mayo (page 264) or store-bought mayonnaise

1 small red onion, finely chopped

3 stalks celery, halved lengthwise and thinly sliced

1 large carrot, peeled, halved lengthwise, and thinly sliced

½ cup quartered purple grapes

1 chipotle pepper in adobo sauce, finely diced

3 tablespoons slivered almonds

2 tablespoons roughly chopped raw cashews

1½ teaspoons coconut aminos

½ teaspoon raw honey

½ teaspoon yellow mustard

Curry powder

Dried dillweed

Ground cumin

Garlic powder

Ground ginger

Fine sea salt

Ground black pepper

1. For the chicken: In a medium bowl, season the chicken with the sea salt and black pepper.

2. Add 1 cup water to an electric pressure cooker and place the trivet inside. Carefully place the chicken breasts on the trivet. Place the lid on the cooker and make sure the vent valve is in the SEALING position. Using the display panel, select the MANUAL/PRESSURE COOK function and HIGH PRESSURE, and use the +/− buttons until the display reads 16 minutes.

3. When the cooker beeps to let you know it's finished, let it naturally release pressure until the display reads LO:15. Switch the vent valve from the SEALING to the VENTING position. Use caution while the steam escapes—it's hot.

4. Remove chicken from the cooker and place in a medium bowl. Shred the chicken using a hand mixer or two forks. Makes 5 cups shredded chicken.

5. Assemble the salads (recipes follow).

Note: Do not throw the broth that is leftover inside the pressure cooker away—that is chicken stock! Save it in a wide-mouth mason jar for up to a week and use in any recipe that calls for chicken or vegetable broth. Makes about 2 cups of broth.

CURRY CHICKEN SALAD

SERVES 2

1 cup shredded cooked chicken

¼ cup thinly sliced celery

¼ cup thinly sliced carrots

3 tablespoons Homemade Mayo (page 264) or store-bought mayonnaise

2 tablespoons roughly chopped raw cashews

2 tablespoons finely chopped red onion

1 teaspoon curry powder

Fine sea salt

Ground black pepper

Using a spoon, mix all the ingredients together in a medium bowl, adding the salt and pepper to taste. Divide the salad into two equal portions and store in the refrigerator for up to 5 days.

dill chicken
salad

curry chicken
salad

CHIPOTLE CHICKEN SALAD

SERVES 2

1 cup shredded cooked chicken

¼ cup thinly sliced carrot

1 chipotle pepper in adobo sauce, finely diced

3 tablespoons Homemade Mayo (page 264) or store-bought mayonnaise

2 tablespoons finely chopped red onion

¼ teaspoon ground cumin

¼ teaspoon garlic powder

Fine sea salt

Ground black pepper

Using a spoon, mix all the ingredients together in a medium bowl, adding the salt and pepper to taste. Divide the salad into two equal portions and store in the refrigerator for up to 5 days.

DILL CHICKEN SALAD

SERVES 2

1 cup shredded cooked chicken

½ cup quartered purple grapes

¼ cup thinly sliced celery

3 tablespoons Homemade Mayo (page 264) or store-bought mayonnaise

2 tablespoons finely chopped red onion

2 tablespoons slivered almonds

1 teaspoon dried dillweed

Fine sea salt

Ground black pepper

Using a spoon, mix all the ingredients together in a medium bowl, adding the salt and pepper to taste. Divide the salad into two equal portions and store in the refrigerator for up to 5 days.

HONEY GINGER CHICKEN SALAD

SERVES 2

1 cup shredded cooked chicken

¼ cup thinly sliced carrot

¼ cup thinly sliced celery

3 tablespoons Homemade Mayo (page 264) or store-bought mayonnaise

2 tablespoons finely chopped red onion

1 tablespoon slivered almonds

1½ teaspoons coconut aminos

½ teaspoon raw honey

⅛ teaspoon ground ginger

⅛ teaspoon garlic powder

Using a spoon, mix all the ingredients together in a medium bowl. Divide the salad into two equal portions and store in the refrigerator for up to 5 days.

DUMP CHICKEN SALAD

SERVES 2

1 cup shredded cooked chicken

3 tablespoons Homemade Mayo (page 264) or store-bought mayonnaise

½ teaspoon yellow mustard

All the leftover celery, carrot, and red onion

Fine sea salt

Ground black pepper

Using a spoon, mix all the ingredients together in a medium bowl, adding the salt and pepper to taste. Divide the salad into two equal portions and store in the refrigerator for up to 5 days.

beef and lamb

Korean Beef

Cowboy Chili

Mini Grass-Fed Burgers with Chipotle Mayo

Healthy Hamburger Mac and Cheese

Sirloin Steak Strips with Mushrooms and Balsamic Glaze

Tangy Barbecue Beef Back Ribs

Steak and Veggie Kabobs

Lamb Rogan Josh

KOREAN BEEF

I used to love getting takeout Asian food. There's something so satisfying and comforting about it, but once I began watching what ingredients went into my food, it became harder for me to order takeout—simply because, most of the time, I have no idea what restaurants put into their food. So, to get around this, I like to mimic my favorite takeout dishes at home. Korean beef is one of my family's favorites. I pair ours with a complex carbohydrate like brown rice. You can also serve this over cauliflower rice or steamed broccoli.

--------- SERVES 4 ---------

1 pound beef tips or cubed beef stew meat

Fine sea salt

Ground black pepper

1 tablespoon sesame oil or extra-virgin olive oil

¼ cup beef or vegetable broth (see page 108)

5 cloves garlic, minced

1 teaspoon freshly grated ginger

2 tablespoons coconut aminos

1 tablespoon raw honey

¼ teaspoon crushed red pepper flakes

¼ cup finely chopped green onions

1 tablespoon sesame seeds

Veggie Brown Rice (page 239) or steamed broccoli

1. Preheat an electric pressure cooker using the SAUTÉ function. Liberally season the beef with sea salt and black pepper.

2. When the display panel reads HOT, add the oil and beef to the cooker. Cook the beef, stirring periodically, until it's browned on all sides, about 5 minutes.

3. Add the beef broth, garlic, ginger, coconut aminos, honey, and red pepper flakes to the pot. Place the lid on the pressure cooker and make sure the vent valve is in the SEALING position. Using the display panel, press the CANCEL button. Select the MANUAL/PRESSURE COOK function and HIGH PRESSURE. Use the +/– buttons until the display reads 30 minutes.

4. When the pot beeps to let you know it's finished, let it naturally release pressure. Or, if you're in a hurry, open the pressure valve and let the remaining steam escape. Top the beef with green onions and sesame seeds and serve alongside veggie brown rice or steamed broccoli.

COWBOY CHILI

Inspired by the typical chilis found in rural Texas, where we lived for several years, this chili reminds me of the special time we spent there. Extra hearty with a healthy dose of spice, make sure you make enough for leftovers because, like most chilis, it tastes even better after spending the night in the fridge!

───────────── **SERVES 6** ─────────────

1 pound beef stew meat, cubed

2 teaspoons fine sea salt

½ teaspoon ground black pepper

1 large yellow onion, diced

1 red bell pepper, seeded and diced

1 medium jalapeño, halved lengthwise and thinly sliced (leave the seeds in for extra spice)

2 tablespoons extra-virgin olive oil

1 (15-ounce) can kidney beans, rinsed and drained

1 (15-ounce) can black beans, rinsed and drained

2 tablespoons chili powder

1½ tablespoons garlic powder

1 tablespoon dried minced onion

2 (15-ounce) cans tomato sauce

1 (15-ounce) can diced tomatoes, undrained

Finely chopped green onions, for serving

Sour cream or plain Greek yogurt, for serving

Golden Sweet Corn Bread (page 80), for serving

1. Preheat an electric pressure cooker using the SAUTÉ function. Season the beef with 1 teaspoon of the sea salt and the black pepper.

2. When the display panel reads HOT, add the beef, onion, bell pepper, jalapeño, and olive oil to the pot. Cook, stirring, until the meat has browned on all sides, about 5 minutes.

3. Add the beans, chili powder, garlic powder, dried onion, and remaining 1 teaspoon sea salt and stir. Then add the tomato sauce and diced tomatoes. DO NOT STIR. If the tomato sauce comes in contact with the bottom of the pot you may receive a burn notice.

4. Place the lid on the pressure cooker. Make sure the vent valve is in the SEALING position. Using the display panel, press the CANCEL button. Select the MANUAL/PRESSURE COOK function and HIGH PRESSURE. Use the +/– buttons until the display reads 30 minutes.

5. When the cooker beeps to let you know it's finished, open the pressure valve and let the steam escape. Be careful—it's hot.

6. Stir the chili and ladle into bowls. Let cool slightly, then serve with green onions, sour cream, and corn bread.

MINI GRASS-FED BURGERS WITH CHIPOTLE MAYO

The trick for making delicious, moist, fall-apart ground beef patties is making sure you don't overwork the meat. The more you knead and mix it, the tougher your patties will be. Less is more with these beauts, so make sure to gently fold in the ingredients, and you'll have melt-in-your-mouth burgers.

MAKES 10 SMALL BURGERS   SERVES 4

1 pound 80% lean grass-fed ground beef

1 large egg

¼ cup finely chopped yellow onion

1 tablespoon reduced-sodium Worcestershire sauce

2 tablespoons gluten-free old-fashioned rolled oats

½ teaspoon garlic powder

⅛ teaspoon cayenne pepper

½ teaspoon fine sea salt

¼ teaspoon ground black pepper

1 tablespoon salted butter or ghee

½ cup Homemade Mayo (page 264) or store-bought mayonnaise

1 chipotle pepper in adobo sauce

1. Preheat an electric griddle to 350°F, or a cast-iron skillet over medium heat.

2. In a large bowl, combine the ground beef, egg, chopped onion, Worcestershire sauce, oats, garlic powder, cayenne pepper, sea salt, and black pepper. Gently mix the ingredients together; do not overwork the meat or it can become tough.

3. Take ¼ cup of the meat mixture and gently form a patty between your palms. Repeat to make 10 small patties.

4. Once the griddle is hot, lightly grease it with the butter. Place the patties on the griddle and cook for 3 minutes on each side, until cooked through. Transfer to a plate and let cool.

5. Prepare the chipotle mayo by combining the mayo with the chipotle pepper in a wide-mouth mason jar. Using an immersion blender, blend on high until the pepper is completely blended with the mayo.

continued on page 170

1 head butterhead lettuce, leaves separated (see Note)

2 Roma tomatoes, sliced

1 medium avocado, pitted, peeled, and sliced

½ small red onion, thinly sliced

½ cup bread-and-butter or dill pickles

6. For each burger wrap, layer two small or medium lettuce leaves to form the bottom of the wrap. Place a patty on top and smear with chipotle mayo, then top with tomato, avocado, onion, and pickles. Place one small or medium lettuce leaf on top to complete your wrap.

Note: Instead of wrapping the patties in lettuce, you can serve the patties in mini versions of the Amazing Flourless Hamburger Buns recipe (page 89). To make eight small mini buns (instead of the four it specifies), divide the dough into 8 balls and place on a lined baking sheet. Wet your hands slightly and shape each dough ball into a 1½ inch round. With a pastry brush or your fingers, smear some of the leftover egg over the tops, then sprinkle with the sesame seeds. Bake for 28 to 32 minutes, until the bun tops are golden brown. Remove to a wire rack and allow to cool completely before slicing.

HEALTHY HAMBURGER MAC AND CHEESE

I enjoy taking food that I used to eat and reinventing it to make it healthier. Just because I don't eat box meals, microwave dinners, or fast food anymore doesn't mean I can't enjoy the same flavors. This is a cheesy, delicious, healthy "hamburger helper" without dairy or gluten. It's also allergy-friendly and kid-friendly and hits the comfort spot!

SERVES 6
---

1 tablespoon extra-virgin olive oil

1 medium yellow onion, diced

1 pound lean 80% lean grass-fed ground beef

5 cloves garlic, minced

3 cups water

1 carrot, peeled and diced

¼ cup unfortified nutritional yeast

1 teaspoon garlic powder

1½ teaspoons fine sea salt

¼ teaspoon ground black pepper

8 ounces gluten-free elbow pasta

2 tablespoons arrowroot flour

1. Preheat an electric pressure cooker using the SAUTÉ function.

2. When the display panel reads HOT, add the olive oil and then the onion. Cook, stirring periodically, for 3 minutes. Add the ground beef and garlic and cook, stirring and crumbling the beef, until it is browned, about 5 minutes.

3. While the meat is browning, combine 3 cups water, the carrot, nutritional yeast, garlic powder, sea salt, and black pepper in a high-powered blender. Blend on high until everything is smooth, about 30 seconds.

4. Pour the contents of the blender over the ground meat in the pressure cooker, then add the elbow pasta and stir. Place the lid on the cooker and make sure the vent valve is in the SEALING position. Using the display panel, press the CANCEL button to turn off the SAUTÉ function, then select the MANUAL/PRESSURE COOK function and HIGH PRESSURE. Use the +/− buttons until the display reads 6 minutes.

5. When the cooker beeps to let you know it's finished, switch the vent valve from the SEALING to the VENTING position, administering a quick release. Use caution while the steam escapes—it's hot.

6. Add the arrowroot flour and stir until the sauce thickens. Serve warm.

SIRLOIN STEAK STRIPS WITH MUSHROOMS AND BALSAMIC GLAZE

Done properly, this is a bit of a fine-dining experience. Brady told me it reminded him of the fancy restaurant my parents took us to celebrate the launch of the first *Instant Loss Cookbook* and, I have to say, I agree. This is fancier than our usual weeknight dinner, and it certainly is fun to make for company. I get my sirloin steak strips at Trader Joe's or Target. If you can't find precut strips, get a sirloin steak and cut your own! Make sure you cut against the grain instead of with it.

SERVES 4

1 pound sirloin steak strips

½ teaspoon fine sea salt

¼ teaspoon ground black pepper

1 tablespoon extra-virgin olive oil

8 ounces white mushrooms, wiped clean and thinly sliced

5 cloves garlic, minced

2 tablespoons coconut aminos

1 tablespoon balsamic vinegar

1 teaspoon fresh squeezed orange juice

1 teaspoon salted butter or ghee

½ teaspoon Dijon mustard

1½ teaspoons arrowroot flour

1 recipe Garlic Mashed Cauliflower (page 244)

1. Preheat an electric pressure cooker using the SAUTÉ function. While you wait for the cooker to warm, toss the steak strips with the sea salt and black pepper.

2. When the display panel reads HOT, add the olive oil and steak strips and cook for 2 minutes, until browned. Flip the strips and brown the other side, about 1 minute. Add the mushrooms, garlic, coconut aminos, balsamic vinegar, orange juice, butter, and Dijon mustard.

3. Place the lid on top and make sure the vent valve is in the SEALING position. Using the display panel, press the CANCEL button, then select MANUAL/PRESSURE COOK and HIGH PRESSURE. Use the +/– buttons until the display reads 15 minutes.

4. When the cooker beeps to let you know it's finished, let it naturally release the pressure until the display reads LO:10. Switch the vent valve from the SEALING to the VENTING position. Use caution while the steam escapes—it's hot.

5. Remove the lid. Using the display panel, press the CANCEL button to turn off the KEEP WARM function, then select the SAUTÉ function. Add the arrowroot flour and stir until the sauce thickens, about 1 minute. Serve the steak strips and mushrooms over the mashed cauliflower.

TANGY BARBECUE BEEF BACK RIBS

I never liked ribs until I started cooking beef ribs in my pressure cooker. If you haven't tried ribs this way, boy are you missing out! The ribs will literally fall off the bone and melt in your mouth. Whether you need something for game day or you just want a finger-licking good dinner, these tasty ribs are a treat!

SERVES 4

2 teaspoons coconut sugar

2 teaspoons chili powder

2 teaspoons dried minced onion

1 tablespoon fine sea salt

2 teaspoons ground black pepper

3½ to 4 pounds bone-in beef back ribs (see Note)

1 cup water

½ cup apple cider vinegar

2 teaspoons liquid smoke

1 cup Tangy Barbecue Sauce (page 268)

1. In a small bowl, combine the coconut sugar, chili powder, dried onion, sea salt, and black pepper. Place the ribs on a large plate and thoroughly coat them with the spice mixture, using your fingers to rub the spices into the meat.

2. Combine 1 cup water, the apple cider vinegar, and liquid smoke in an electric pressure cooker and set the trivet inside. Carefully place the rack of ribs on the trivet. If they do not fit, cut them in half.

3. Place the lid on the cooker and make sure the vent valve is in the SEALING position. Using the display panel, select the MANUAL/PRESSURE COOK function and HIGH PRESSURE, and use the +/− buttons until the display reads 55 minutes.

4. When the cooker beeps to let you know it's finished, switch the vent valve from the SEALING to the VENTING position, administering a quick release. Use caution while the steam escapes—it's hot.

5. Turn on the broiler in the oven. Remove the ribs from the cooker and place on a baking sheet. Slather with the barbecue sauce. Place under the broiler to brown for 4 to 5 minutes. Let cool for 5 minutes and serve warm.

Note: Do not throw your bones away! Save the bones in the freezer to make a beautiful bone broth: Add the bones to the pressure cooker with some water, apple cider vinegar, favorite herbs, and vegetables (see page 108).

STEAK AND VEGGIE KABOBS

We live in the desert and don't have AC on the bottom floor of our house. For that reason, I avoid turning on anything that will make the house warmer during the summer. We grill outside, or use the air fryer or electric pressure cooker—anything to avoid turning on the oven. Kabobs made in the air fryer is a great example of summertime ovenless cooking. If you don't have an air fryer, use your grill or the oven instructions below.

SERVES 2

2 tablespoons extra-virgin olive oil

2 teaspoons reduced-sodium Worcestershire sauce

½ teaspoon fresh lemon juice

1 teaspoon fresh thyme leaves

¼ teaspoon fine sea salt

¼ teaspoon ground black pepper

8 ounces beef tenderloin, cut into 1-inch chunks

1 small zucchini, cut into large chunks

4 medium button mushrooms

½ orange bell pepper, seeded and cut into large chunks

½ red onion, cut into large chunks

6 to 8 (6-inch) wooden skewers

1. In a large bowl, combine the olive oil, Worcestershire, lemon juice, thyme, sea salt, and black pepper. Add the beef, zucchini, mushrooms, bell pepper, and onion and toss with the marinade. Let sit for 5 to 10 minutes.

2. You want to skewer the meat and vegetables separately: Divide the meat among two or three skewers, then skewer an assortment of vegetables on the other skewers.

3. Add the vegetable skewers to the basket of a 5.3-quart air fryer and bake for 6 minutes at 400°F (see Note).

4. When the air fryer beeps to signal it's finished, place the steak kabobs on top of the vegetables. Bake for 5 minutes at 400°F for medium-rare to medium meat. If you like it more medium to medium-well, cook for an additional minute.

5. Remove the skewers with tongs and divide among plates for serving.

Note: To cook the vegetables and ribs in a conventional oven, roast the veggie kabobs on a baking sheet at 450°F for 15 minutes, flipping once halfway through. Add the meat skewers to the baking sheet and continue to bake, flipping once, for 5 to 6 minutes for medium-rare to medium, or 7 to 8 minutes for medium-well.

LAMB ROGAN JOSH

This aromatic Indian-inspired lamb dish is essentially a curry. It has hunks of meat and a gravy-like sauce. I love to serve this rogan josh over rice with a bit of Greek yogurt and a sprinkle of cilantro.

SERVES 4

2 tablespoons tomato paste

½-inch piece fresh ginger, minced

2 cloves garlic, minced

2 teaspoons garam masala

½ teaspoon ground cumin

½ teaspoon chili powder

¼ teaspoon smoked paprika

¼ teaspoon turmeric

⅛ teaspoon plus ¼ teaspoon fine sea salt

1 tablespoon avocado oil

1 pound boneless leg of lamb, excess fat trimmed, cut into 1-inch cubes

⅛ teaspoon ground black pepper

1 Roma tomato, cored and diced

1 small carrot, peeled and finely chopped

½ large yellow onion, finely chopped

1¼ cups chicken broth or stock (see page 108)

½ cup tomato sauce

¼ cup red lentils

Steamed rice, for serving

½ cup fresh cilantro leaves (optional), for serving

¼ cup Greek yogurt (optional), for serving

1. Preheat an electric pressure cooker using the SAUTÉ function.

2. In a small bowl, combine the tomato paste, ginger, garlic, garam masala, cumin, chili powder, smoked paprika, turmeric, and ⅛ teaspoon of the sea salt. Mix together with a spoon and set aside.

3. When the display panel reads HOT, add the avocado oil and lamb to the cooker. Season with the remaining ¼ teaspoon sea salt and the pepper. Let cook for 5 minutes, stirring periodically, then add the tomato paste mixture, tomato, carrot, onion, chicken broth, tomato sauce, and lentils and stir well to combine.

4. Place the lid on the cooker and make sure the vent valve is in the SEALING position. Using the display panel, press the CANCEL button to turn off the SAUTÉ function, then select MANUAL/PRESSURE COOK function and HIGH PRESSURE. Use the +/− buttons until the display reads 30 minutes.

5. When the cooker beeps to let you know it's finished, switch the vent valve from the SEALING to the VENTING position, administering a quick release. Use caution while the steams escapes—it's hot!

6. Ladle the rogan josh over steamed rice and garnish with fresh cilantro and a dollop of yogurt, if desired. Serve with a side salad.

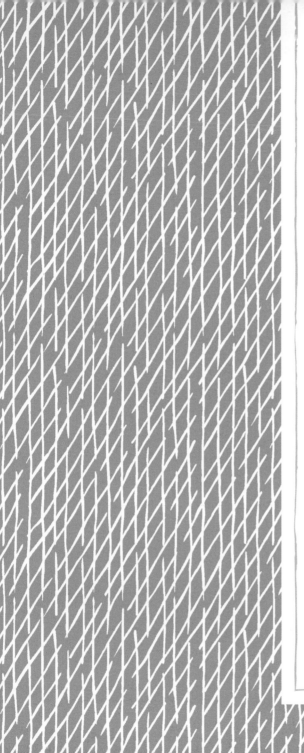

seafood

Blackened Salmon with Pineapple Avocado Salsa

Fish and Chips for Two

Salmon en Papillote with Mango Curry and Broccoli Mash

Mango Mahi-Mahi BBQ Fish Tacos

Summer Shrimp Quinoa

Jicama Tostadas with Citrus Crab Salad and Avocado Cream

Coconut Fried Shrimp with Sweet Chili Mint Sauce

Fresh Herb Tuna Salad

BLACKENED SALMON WITH PINEAPPLE AVOCADO SALSA

Those of you who know me know that I was never a fish girl. I was such a picky eater, the thought of eating raw vegetables and fish literally made me shudder. Part of becoming healthier for me was regenerating my taste buds. Did you know that taste buds regenerate every 10 to 14 days? Meaning, if you don't like something, you can actually train yourself to like it? I was skeptical, but I didn't really have any other options. I had to figure out a way to enjoy the foods I didn't like. I soon discovered that I actually did like some foods I thought I didn't when I found ways to prepare them to suit my preferences. Blackened salmon is one example. I use fresh, wild-caught salmon, which is much less fishy than farmed. And I serve it with a fresh and light pineapple avocado salsa. Put the two in a corn tortilla, and you're in for a real treat!

SERVES 2

2 (4-ounce) wild-caught salmon fillets, scales and pin bones removed

½ lime

½ teaspoon chili powder

½ teaspoon fine sea salt

¼ teaspoon cayenne pepper

2 tablespoons salted butter or ghee

Pineapple Avocado Salsa (page 184)

1. Heat a cast-iron skillet over high heat.

2. Spritz the salmon fillets with lime juice. In a small bowl, combine the chili powder, sea salt, and cayenne. Rub the seasonings into the pink part of the fillets.

3. Melt the butter in the hot skillet, then place the salmon, skin-side down, in the pan and cook until blackened on one side, 3 to 5 minutes. Flip and cook the other side for about 2 minutes. You'll know the fish is done when it's just a little pink and flakes easily with a fork. Serve with the salsa.

PINEAPPLE AVOCADO SALSA

1 ripe medium avocado, pitted, peeled, and diced

1 small jalapeño, diced

½ small red onion, diced

1 cup diced pineapple

1 tablespoon chopped fresh cilantro leaves

1½ teaspoons lime juice

2 teaspoons avocado oil

¼ teaspoon fine sea salt

⅛ teaspoon ground black pepper

Combine all ingredients in a bowl and toss. Serve with the blackened salmon or tacos, or enjoy it with Air Fryer Tortilla Chips (page 277). Store in the refrigerator for up to 2 days.

FISH AND CHIPS FOR TWO

This cod will melt in your mouth, *like butter*. My husband has always enjoyed going to pubs with his coworkers, and ordering fish and chips is his how he gauges the quality of their menu. This recipe lands high on his list of favorite fish and chips platters. The chips and fish are both made inside the air fryer basket (see Note), which makes for easy cleanup!

SERVES 2

2 small sweet potatoes (about 8 ounces), peeled and cut into thin shoestring strips

1 tablespoon avocado oil, plus more for brushing

½ teaspoon fine sea salt

¼ teaspoon ground black pepper

2 tablespoons coconut flour

1 tablespoon arrowroot flour

½ teaspoon garlic powder

1 large egg

1 (8-ounce) wild-caught cod fillet, cut into 1-inch strips

¼ cup Lemon Caper Tartar Sauce (page 187)

1. In a bowl, toss the sweet potatoes with the avocado oil, ¼ teaspoon of the sea salt, and ⅛ teaspoon of the black pepper. Spread the potatoes evenly in a single layer in a 5.3-quart air fryer basket. Bake for 9 minutes at 370°F.

2. While the sweet potatoes fries are baking, combine the coconut flour, arrowroot flour, garlic powder, and remaining ¼ teaspoon sea salt and ⅛ teaspoon black pepper in a shallow bowl. In a separate bowl, whisk the egg until it becomes light and frothy.

3. Take a strip of cod with one hand, dip both sides in the egg, then use your other (dry) hand to dredge in the flour mixture to coat. Repeat until all the strips are coated. Using a silicone brush, lightly brush both sides of each strip with avocado oil; or spray cooking spray on each side instead.

4. When the air fryer beeps to signal it's finished, move all the sweet potato fries to a corner of the fryer basket. You will need to stack them on top of each other so that all the pieces of cod will fit. Layer the cod in a single layer on the bottom of the fryer. Then place the basket inside the cooker and cook for 10 minutes at 370°F, turning the fish over once halfway through the cook time.

5. Divide the fish and chips into two equal portions and serve with a side of tartar sauce.

continued on page 187

LEMON CAPER TARTAR SAUCE

3 tablespoons Homemade Mayo (page 264) or store-bought mayonnaise

½ teaspoon freshly grated lemon zest

1½ teaspoons fresh lemon juice

1 teaspoon capers, drained and finely chopped

⅛ teaspoon dried dillweed

Mix all ingredients in a bowl. Store the sauce, covered, in the refrigerator for up to 4 days.

Note: I definitely recommend using an air fryer here, as things don't get nearly as crispy in the oven. However, if you don't have an air fryer, you can bake the fish and chips in a 450°F oven. Bake the chips for 35 to 40 minutes, turning halfway through. Remove from the oven and transfer the chips to a plate. Place the cod on the baking sheet and bake for 12 minutes, turning halfway through.

SALMON EN PAPILLOTE WITH MANGO CURRY AND BROCCOLI MASH

Don't let the fancy name scare you away, *en papillote* is simply French for "in parchment." When you cook something like fish in a parchment paper packet, you're steaming it with its own moisture, so no added fat is required. The mango curry adds a delicious and fresh change to the salmon flavors.

SERVES 4

---

3 cloves garlic, minced

1½ teaspoons finely grated fresh ginger

1 tablespoon coconut aminos

½ teaspoon fresh squeezed lemon juice

¼ teaspoon sriracha or red chili sauce

½ teaspoon curry powder

¼ teaspoon turmeric

4 (4-ounce) wild-caught salmon fillets, scales and pin bones removed

1 cup diced mango

1 cup water

1 pound frozen broccoli florets

1 tablespoon salted butter or ghee

¼ teaspoon fine sea salt

⅛ teaspoon ground black pepper

1. In a small bowl, combine the garlic, ginger, coconut aminos, lemon juice, sriracha, curry powder, and turmeric.

2. Take two large pieces of parchment paper, about 12 inches each, and fold each in half. Unfold and place two salmon fillets on the bottom half of each piece of paper. Coat the fillets with the garlic mixture and top with the mango. Fold the other half of the parchment over the top. Starting on one side, begin to tightly crimp the edges together to form a sealed packet. Once you get to the end, twist the ends of the paper tightly to hold everything together.

3. Add 1 cup water to an electric pressure cooker and place the trivet inside. Carefully place the parchment packets on the trivet. Place the broccoli florets on top of the packets; it's okay if some of the florets fall down the side.

4. Place the lid on the cooker and make sure the vent valve is in the SEALING position. Using the display panel, select the STEAM function and HIGH PRESSURE, and use the +/− buttons until the display reads 3 minutes.

5. When the cooker beeps to let you know it's finished, switch the vent valve from the SEALING to the VENTING position, administering a quick release. Use caution while the steam escapes—it's hot.

6. Remove the broccoli florets and transfer to a medium bowl. Add the butter, sea salt, and black pepper and mash with a fork to combine.

7. Carefully lift the salmon packets out of the pressure cooker and transfer to a plate. Using a knife, cut an opening in the center of each packet and peel the paper away. Then, with a spatula, place a piece of salmon on each plate and spoon the mango and sauce from the packets over the top. Serve with the broccoli mash.

MANGO MAHI-MAHI BBQ FISH TACOS

These vibrant little summer tacos are just flat-out delicious. If you're in a hurry and don't have time to make the barbecue sauce, mayo, corn tortillas, and/or guacamole, you can always use store-bought. Make sure you look for organic, GMO-free corn tortillas, a mayo made with a healthier oil like avocado oil (instead of canola), and a barbecue sauce that doesn't have high fructose corn syrup. But if you have the time to go the extra mile for this recipe, it's worth it!

SERVES 4

1 cup diced fresh or frozen mango

½ cup Tangy Barbecue Sauce (page 268)

4 (4-ounce) fresh skinless mahi-mahi fillets

1 cup water

2 tablespoons Homemade Mayo (page 264) or store-bought mayonnaise

1 teaspoon freshly grated lime zest

1½ cups shredded purple cabbage

1½ cups and shredded peeled carrots (about 5 carrots)

4 green onions, finely chopped

8 Three-Ingredient Corn Tortillas (page 281) or store-bought corn tortillas, warmed

½ cup fresh cilantro leaves

½ cup Best Guacamole Ever (page 269)

1 lime, cut into quarters

1. Combine ½ cup of the mango and the barbecue sauce in a blender or a food processor and process on high until smooth, about 60 seconds.

2. Take two large pieces of parchment paper, about 12 inches each, and fold each in half. Unfold and place two mahi-mahi fillets on the bottom half of each piece of paper. Coat each fillet with 1 tablespoon of the mango barbecue sauce. Fold the other half of the parchment over the top. Starting on one side, begin to tightly crimp the edges together to form a sealed packet. Once you get to the end, twist the ends of the paper tightly to hold everything together.

3. Add 1 cup water to an electric pressure cooker and place the trivet inside. Carefully place the parchment paper packets on the trivet.

4. Place the lid on the cooker and make sure the vent valve is in the SEALING position. Using the display panel, select the MANUAL/PRESSURE COOK function and HIGH PRESSURE, and use the +/− buttons until the display reads 5 minutes.

5. While the fish is cooking, combine the remaining mango barbecue sauce with the mayo and lime zest in a medium bowl. Add the remaining ½ cup diced mango, the cabbage, carrots, and green onions and toss to coat. Chill the mango slaw in the fridge until the fish is done cooking.

6. When the cooker beeps to let you know it's finished, switch the vent valve from the SEALING to the VENTING position, administering a quick release. Use caution while the steam escapes, it's hot.

7. Using a knife, cut an opening in the center of each packet and peel the paper away. Then, with a fork, flake the fish and serve in corn tortillas with the mango slaw, fresh cilantro, and a scoop of guacamole. Spritz the top of each taco with a squeeze of lime.

SUMMER SHRIMP QUINOA

This light, tasty summertime dish is a hit when brought to picnics or potlucks. When eating a meal paired with a seed or a grain like quinoa or rice, I like to enjoy a Simple House Salad (page 122) first so that I'm not tempted to eat more than a fair portion. Ideally, you only want to eat ¾ to 1 cup quinoa. Even though it's a healthy and excellent source of plant-based protein, it's also a little heavy and something I try to portion correctly while I'm losing weight.

SERVES 4 TO 6

---

1 pound extra-large or jumbo shrimp (21–30 count), peeled and deveined

½ pound fresh asparagus, woody ends removed, cut into 2-inch pieces

1 cup quinoa, rinsed and drained

1 cup chicken broth or stock (see page 108)

¼ cup thinly sliced red onion

2 tablespoons extra-virgin olive oil

2 tablespoons white wine vinegar

2 cloves garlic, minced

2 teaspoons minced fresh stemmed dill

¾ teaspoon fine sea salt

¼ teaspoon ground black pepper

½ cup frozen baby peas

½ cup diced Roma tomatoes

4 to 6 lemon wedges

1. Combine the shrimp, asparagus, quinoa, chicken broth, red onion, olive oil, white vinegar, garlic, dill, sea salt, and black pepper in an electric pressure cooker and stir. Place the lid on the pot and make sure the vent valve is in the SEALING position. Using the display panel, select the STEAM function and HIGH PRESSURE, and use the +/− buttons until the display reads 1 minute.

2. When the cooker beeps to let you know it's finished, let it naturally release pressure until the display reads LO:10. Switch the vent valve from the SEALING to the VENTING position. Use caution while the steam escapes—it's hot.

3. Stir in the baby peas and tomatoes. (The peas will thaw in about 30 seconds.) Serve warm with lemon wedges for spritzing.

JICAMA TOSTADAS WITH CITRUS CRAB SALAD AND AVOCADO CREAM

No cooking required! I try to make at least one no-cook meal a day. The benefits of a raw diet are immense, but there's also something beautiful and special about a dish made out of all raw ingredients! This is a go-to meal in the summertime for us. Fresh crab meat is preferred, but that can be difficult to find. Canned crab meat is a bit more accessible and available in most supermarkets—you'll find it in a 6- or 8-ounce cans. Don't worry, if you can't find exactly 8 ounces, just get close.

SERVES 4

FOR THE CRAB SALAD

8 ounces fresh or canned claw or lump crab meat, drained and picked through for shells

2 tablespoons finely chopped red onion

2 tablespoons finely chopped seeded red bell pepper

2 tablespoons fresh orange juice

1 tablespoon fresh lime juice

1 tablespoon chopped fresh flat-leaf parsley leaves

½ teaspoon finely chopped jalapeño

⅛ teaspoon fine sea salt

FOR THE JICAMA "TOSTADAS"

1 jicama (4-inch diameter), ends removed and peeled

FOR THE AVOCADO CREAM

1 ripe medium avocado, pitted and peeled

2 tablespoons avocado oil

1 teaspoon fresh lime juice

¼ teaspoon fine sea salt

⅛ teaspoon ground black pepper

4 to 8 lime wedges

1. For the crab salad: Combine all the ingredients in a bowl. Mix everything together gently to keep the crab from breaking apart too much. Set aside to marinate.

2. For the tostadas: With a mandoline or sharp knife, carefully slice the jicama into $1/8$-inch-thick rounds.

3. For the avocado cream: In a small bowl, mash the avocado well with a fork. Stir in the avocado oil, lime juice, sea salt, and black pepper.

4. To assemble, place a jicama slice on a plate. Spoon a hearty tablespoon of avocado cream on the jicama and top with 2 tablespoons crab salad. Squeeze a little lime juice over the top and enjoy.

COCONUT FRIED SHRIMP WITH SWEET CHILI MINT SAUCE

This is one of my top-five favorite recipes in this book. I've mentioned it many times, but I used to be a picky kid who hated all things seafood. After I started to retrain my taste buds, things like salmon and cod were easy to incorporate, but I still had a heck of a time trying to stomach shrimp . . . until this recipe. OMG y'all: Make sure there's someone around to share this dish with or you just might eat the whole thing by yourself. I might be speaking from personal experience . . .

If you cannot find the exact size shrimp, a similar size can be used. And you can use frozen or fresh—if using frozen make sure to thaw the shrimp completely before using.

— SERVES 4 —

½ cup coconut flour

1 teaspoon fine sea salt

½ teaspoon ground black pepper

2 large eggs

1½ cups unsweetened shredded coconut

1 pound jumbo shrimp (21–25 count), peeled and deveined

Avocado or coconut oil cooking spray

Sweet Chili Mint Sauce (page 198)

1. In a shallow bowl, combine the coconut flour, sea salt, and black pepper with a spoon. In a second bowl, whisk the eggs. In a third bowl, spread out the shredded coconut.

2. Working in batches, add a few shrimp to the flour and toss to coat. Shake off any excess flour and add to the bowl with beaten egg. Coat the shrimp on all sides with egg and then transfer to the bowl with the coconut. Using a dry hand, roll the shrimp around until the coconut completely covers the shrimp, then set on a large plate. Repeat until all of the shrimp have been coated.

3. Remove the fryer basket and coat the bottom with the cooking spray. Place half of the shrimp in the basket and spray the tops with cooking oil. Do not skip this step as this is what makes the shrimp crispy. If you do not have cooking spray, use a silicone brush to brush avocado oil on the shrimp.

continued on page 198

4. Bake the shrimp at 370°F for 4 minutes (see Note). Flip the shrimp with tongs, and cook for another 4 minutes on the other side, until the shrimp are golden. Repeat for the second batch.

5. Serve hot with sweet chili mint sauce.

Note: You can also bake the shrimp in a conventional oven. Preheat the oven to 350°F and set a cooling rack in a baking sheet. Transfer all the coated shrimp to the baking sheet and coat with cooking oil spray. Bake for 10 minutes, flipping the shrimp halfway through and coating with more cooking spray, until the shrimp are golden.

SWEET CHILI MINT SAUCE

Do not skip the sauce; it makes such a wonderful pairing with the shrimp. It's an absolute must!

MAKES ½ CUP

1 small jalapeño with seeds, roughly chopped

5 tablespoons 100% pure maple syrup

2 tablespoons rice wine vinegar

2 cloves garlic, roughly chopped

1 tablespoon finely chopped fresh mint

Combine all the ingredients except the mint in a wide-mouth mason jar. Blend on low with an immersion blender until the sauce is well blended. Stir in the mint. Store covered in the refrigerator for up to a week.

FRESH HERB TUNA SALAD

Tuna salad is something simple we eat often for lunch. It literally takes five minutes to put together! I like to serve it over salad or rice cakes, and it's fun to eat it as a dip with plantain chips.

───────────────── SERVES 4 ─────────────────

2 (5-ounce) cans solid white albacore tuna, drained and shredded

½ cup Homemade Mayo (page 264) or store-bought mayonnaise

1 teaspoon fresh squeezed lemon juice

½ teaspoon curry powder

⅛ teaspoon fine ground black pepper

1 tablespoon chopped fresh chives

1 tablespoon chopped fresh flat-leaf parsley

1 teaspoon chopped fresh dill

Combine the tuna, mayo, lemon juice, curry powder, and black pepper in a large bowl and stir to combine. Add the chives, parsley, and dill and stir again. Store in the refrigerator for up to 3 days.

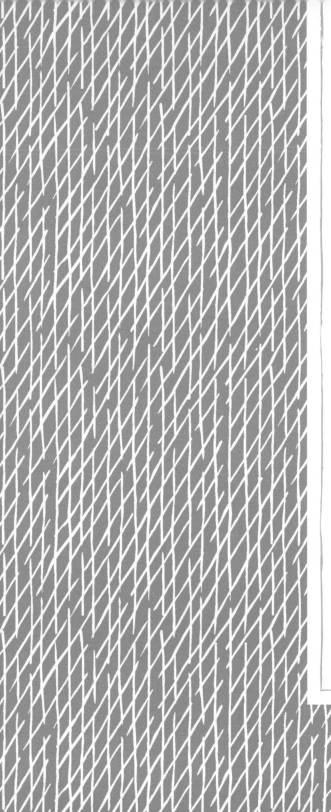

pork

Roasted Eggplant with Pork Ragu

Bacon-Wrapped Pork Tenderloin with Fried Apples and Honey Sriracha Glaze

Pork Carnitas Tacos

Pork with Herb au Jus

Italian Stuffed Bell Peppers

ROASTED EGGPLANT WITH PORK RAGU

Eggplant is a great versatile vegetable. It can be used like a noodle in certain recipes, which is really cool! This recipe is basically a deconstructed lasagna. Incredibly tasty, it's a great feel-good meal.

--- SERVES 4 ---

FOR THE PORK RAGU

¾ pound boneless pork shoulder, excess fat trimmed, cut into ½-inch cubes

1 small yellow onion, finely diced

1 tablespoon extra-virgin olive oil

4 ounces white mushrooms, finely chopped

3 cloves garlic, minced

1 cup tomato sauce

1 cup canned diced tomatoes (undrained)

2 tablespoons tomato paste

1½ teaspoons balsamic vinegar

½ teaspoon dried basil

½ teaspoon dried oregano

½ teaspoon dried thyme

¼ teaspoon fine sea salt

⅛ teaspoon ground black pepper

1. Preheat the oven to 475°F. Line a baking sheet with parchment paper.

2. For the pork ragu: Preheat an electric pressure cooker using the SAUTÉ function. When the display panel reads HOT, add the olive oil, pork, and onion. Cook, stirring occasionally, for 5 minutes. Add the mushrooms, garlic, tomato sauce, diced tomatoes, tomato paste, balsamic vinegar, dried basil, oregano, thyme, sea salt, and black pepper and stir.

3. Place the lid on the cooker and make sure the vent valve is in the SEALING position. Using the display panel, press the CANCEL button to turn off the SAUTÉ function. Select MANUAL/PRESSURE COOK function and HIGH PRESSURE, and use the +/− buttons until the display reads 30 minutes.

continued on page 206

FOR THE EGGPLANT

1 medium eggplant, peeled and sliced into 1-inch rounds

3 tablespoons extra-virgin olive oil

¼ teaspoon fine sea salt

¼ teaspoon ground black pepper

FOR THE "CHEESE" SAUCE

1 large egg

½ cup raw cashews

¼ cup unsweetened almond milk

¼ cup unfortified nutritional yeast

¼ teaspoon fine sea salt

⅛ teaspoon ground black pepper

1 to 2 tablespoons chopped fresh basil, for garnish

4. For the eggplant: Arrange the eggplant slices on the lined baking sheet, brush each side with about ½ teaspoon of the olive oil, and season with the sea salt and black pepper. Bake in the oven for 20 minutes, flipping the eggplant over halfway through, until the eggplant is tender.

5. While the ragu and eggplant cook, prepare the cheese sauce: Combine the egg, cashews, almond milk, nutritional yeast, sea salt, and black pepper in a high-powered blender and blend on high for 5 minutes. Transfer to a bowl and set aside.

6. After the eggplant has baked for 20 minutes, spoon cheese sauce evenly over the top of each eggplant slice and bake for 5 minutes longer, until the "cheese" has browned.

7. When the cooker beeps to let you know it's finished, switch the vent valve from the SEALING to the VENTING position, administering a quick release. Use caution while the steams escapes—it's hot.

8. Slice the eggplant into ¼-inch slices (or leave whole—it's up to you!) and divide among four plates. Ladle the pork ragu over the eggplant, sprinkle with fresh basil, and serve.

BACON-WRAPPED PORK TENDERLOIN WITH FRIED APPLES AND HONEY SRIRACHA GLAZE

The air fryer really works wonders with bacon-wrapped pork. The bacon comes out so crisp, and its fat cooks the pork to perfection. I'll never make a tenderloin in the oven again! The glaze adds just the right amount of sweet and spice to make this a staple pork recipe.

— SERVES 4 —

8 ounces (8 to 12 slices) thin-cut nitrate-free bacon

1 pound pork tenderloin, fat and silverskin removed

¼ teaspoon garlic powder

¼ teaspoon fine sea salt

⅛ fine ground black pepper

¼ cup raw honey

1 tablespoon sriracha

1 large Gala red apple, cored and cut into 8 wedges

1. On a cutting board, lay out the strips of bacon lengthwise, overlapping slightly, so that there will be enough bacon to completely wrap the tenderloin. Place the tenderloin in the center of the bacon.

2. In a small bowl, combine the garlic powder, sea salt, and pepper. Rub the spice mixture into the pork. Fold the bacon over the pork and roll it up to form a neat package. Put the pork in the air fryer basket seam side down and bake at 400°F for 10 minutes (see Note).

3. In a small bowl, whisk together the honey and sriracha. Set aside 2 tablespoons of the glaze for serving.

4. When the air fryer beeps to signal that it's finished, flip the tenderloin over with tongs and place the apple wedges around it. Cook at 400°F for another 10 minutes. Brush the pork loin with the remaining honey sriracha glaze and cook for 2 minutes longer, until an instant read thermometer inserted into the pork reads 140°F to 145°F.

5. Using tongs, transfer the pork and apple slices to a cutting board. Cover with foil and let rest 5 to 10 minutes, during which time the internal temperature of the pork will rise a few degrees. There should be a slight hint of pink when you cut into the pork.

6. Slice the pork into eight pieces and serve with the apples and reserved glaze.

Note: You can also bake the wrapped tenderloin in a conventional oven. Bake in a 425°F oven for 10 minutes, flip, and bake for another 12 minutes. Glaze the loin and cook until an instant read thermometer reads 140°F to 145°F, about 3 minutes longer.

PORK CARNITAS TACOS

It's easy to get stuck in a rut, making the same ten recipes over and over again until everyone gets burned out. We eat tacos often, but I try to spice them up (literally) with different meats and seasonings so it's a meal I know everyone will enjoy, but is different enough that it doesn't feel like we're having the same old thing every time.

SERVES 4 TO 6

1 pound boneless pork sirloin, cut into 1-inch pieces (see Note)

1 teaspoon fine sea salt

¼ teaspoon ground black pepper

1 tablespoon extra-virgin olive oil

1 medium orange, halved and seeded

1 medium yellow onion, thinly sliced

1 jalapeño, thinly sliced

3 cloves garlic, minced

1 teaspoon ground cumin

1 teaspoon dried oregano

12 Three-Ingredient Corn Tortillas (page 281) or store-bought corn tortillas

2 cups shredded green leaf lettuce

2 Roma tomatoes, cored and diced

4 radishes, thinly sliced

1 large ripe avocado pitted, peeled, and cut into ¼-inch slices

Sugar-free hot sauce, like El Pato (yellow can), for serving

Lime wedges, for serving

1. In a medium bowl, toss the pork with the sea salt and black pepper. Pour the olive oil in an electric pressure cooker and place the pork on top. Juice the orange halves into the pot and add the spent orange halves, the onion, jalapeño, garlic, cumin, and oregano.

2. Place the lid on the cooker and make sure the vent valve is in the SEALING position. Using the display panel, select the MANUAL/PRESSURE COOK function and HIGH PRESSURE, and use the +/– buttons until the display reads 12 minutes.

3. When the cooker beeps to let you know it's finished, switch the vent valve from the SEALING to the VENTING position, administering a quick release. Use caution while the steam escapes—it's hot.

4. Remove the orange halves and stir the pork. Let the carnitas sit for 10 minutes before serving.

5. Fill each corn tortilla with ¼ cup of the carnitas and garnish with lettuce, tomato, radish, and avocado. Top with your favorite hot sauce and serve with a spritz of lime juice.

Note: If you can't find boneless pork sirloin in your grocery store, substitute pork loin.

PORK WITH HERBS AU JUS

This old-school, classic dinner favorite is a quick protein I can toss inside the pressure cooker on evenings when I just want something quick and filling for the kids. I love to pair it with Garlic Mashed Cauliflower (page 244) or Darn Good Green Beans (page 250).

SERVES 4

1 pound boneless pork loin chops

½ cup chicken broth or stock (see page 108)

2 cloves garlic, minced

1½ teaspoons garlic powder

1 teaspoon dried oregano

1 teaspoon dried basil

1 teaspoon fine sea salt

½ teaspoon ground black pepper

1. Combine all the ingredients in an electric pressure cooker.

2. Place the lid on the cooker and make sure the vent valve is in the SEALING position. Using the display panel, select the MANUAL/PRESSURE COOK function and HIGH PRESSURE, and use the +/– buttons until the display reads 8 minutes.

3. When the cooker beeps to let you know it's finished, let it naturally release pressure until the display reads LO:15. Switch the vent valve from the SEALING to the VENTING position. Use caution while the steam escapes—it's hot.

4. Transfer the pork to a cutting board and slice into ½-inch pieces. Divide the pork evenly among four plates and drizzle each serving with the pot juices (herb au jus).

ITALIAN STUFFED BELL PEPPERS

These delicious little peppers taste exactly like pizza, oddly enough! My husband isn't a bell pepper fan but he really enjoys these—I call that a big win! When purchasing Italian sausage, make sure to check the ingredients. You don't want any artificial colors, added sugars, or MSG.

SERVES 4
---

1 pound Italian sausage meat

1 teaspoon garlic powder

1 teaspoon dried minced onion

¼ teaspoon red pepper flakes

¼ teaspoon fine sea salt

⅛ teaspoon ground black pepper

1 (15-ounce) can diced tomatoes, drained

4 medium to large red bell peppers, tops, stems, and seeds removed

¼ cup shredded mozzarella cheese (optional)

½ cup grated Parmesan cheese (optional)

1 cup water

1. Heat a large cast-iron skillet over medium-high heat. Add the sausage and season with the garlic powder, dried onion, red pepper flakes, sea salt, and black pepper. Cook until the sausage is browned, 6 minutes. Add the diced tomatoes and stir to combine.

2. Stuff the peppers with the sausage mixture and top with mozzarella and Parmesan cheese, if desired.

3. Insert the trivet and add 1 cup of water to an electric pressure cooker. Set the bell peppers upright on the trivet (see Note).

4. Place the lid on the cooker and make sure the vent valve is in the SEALING position. Using the display panel, select the MANUAL/PRESSURE COOK function and HIGH PRESSURE, and use the +/− buttons until the display reads 15 minutes.

5. When the cooker beeps to let you know it's finished, let it naturally release pressure until the display reads LO:10. Switch the vent valve from the SEALING to the VENTING position. Use caution while the steam escapes—it's hot.

6. Carefully lift the peppers out of the pressure cooker using tongs. Serve warm.

Note: You can also make these in your air fryer! Cover the tops of the peppers with foil and bake for 10 minutes at 370°F. Remove the foil and bake for 10 minutes longer to let the cheese brown.

meat-free mains

Roasted Zucchini and Tomatoes with Creamy Garlic Sauce

Super Sloppy Joes

The Ultimate Veggie Burger with Basil Pesto Aioli

Veggie Spring Rolls

Crispy Orange Cauliflower

Summer Zucchini Pasta

Spicy Thai Pizza

Butternut Squash Chipotle Chili

ROASTED ZUCCHINI AND TOMATOES WITH CREAMY GARLIC SAUCE

This is a yummy yet simple little meal that really satisfies my craving for Italian. If you have a loaf of Whole Grain Sandwich Bread (page 86) handy, toast up a few pieces to serve alongside. It's great to have a little bread to soak up all that lovely sauce.

SERVES 4

8 small zucchini (about 2 pounds), ends trimmed

1 cup cherry tomatoes

2 tablespoons extra-virgin olive oil

1½ teaspoons fine sea salt

1 medium yellow onion, diced

8 cloves garlic, minced

3 tablespoons arrowroot flour

⅛ teaspoon ground black pepper

1 cup Hemp Milk (page 266) or almond milk or other milk of choice

1 cup canned full-fat coconut milk

1. Brush the zucchini and cherry tomatoes with 1½ tablespoons of the olive oil, then sprinkle with ½ teaspoon of the sea salt. Place inside a 5.3-quart air fryer basket and bake at 400°F for 15 minutes, turning the zucchini and tomatoes over halfway through, until tender.

2. Heat a large cast-iron skillet over medium-high heat.

3. Once the skillet is hot, add the remaining ½ tablespoon olive oil and the onion and cook, stirring, until the onion begins to soften and become translucent, 2 to 3 minutes. Add the garlic, arrowroot flour, remaining 1 teaspoon sea salt, and the black pepper and mix to combine. Add the hemp milk and coconut milk and cook, stirring continuously, until the mixture begins to bubble and thicken. Continue to cook and stir for 3 to 5 minutes, until a thick sauce forms. Remove the pan from the heat. If you like a smooth sauce, transfer to a blender and blend on high until smooth.

4. While the zucchini is still inside the air fryer basket, use tongs to squeeze out any excess water. The zucchini should flatten a bit. Place two zucchini on each plate, top with the garlic sauce and cherry tomatoes, and serve warm.

SUPER SLOPPY JOES

I'd classify this one as pure kid food. Growing up, my mom would buy sloppy joe mix in a can and microwave it for us, serving it over white hamburger buns for Sloppy Joe Night—always a fun dinner. Just because I don't eat it on white bread or out of a can anymore, doesn't mean I can't have it at all! This is a super easy dump meal, really. Just toss everything inside the pressure cooker and let it work its magic. It's almost as easy as microwaving!

SERVES 4 TO 6

1 small red onion, diced

1 cup lentils, rinsed and drained

1 green bell pepper, seeded and diced

½ cup vegetable or chicken stock

1 (15-ounce) can tomato sauce

2 tablespoons reduced-sodium Worcestershire sauce

2 tablespoons 100% pure maple syrup

1 tablespoon plus 1 teaspoon red wine vinegar

½ teaspoon paprika

½ teaspoon chili powder

½ teaspoon garlic powder

½ teaspoon dried minced onion

½ teaspoon fine sea salt

¼ teaspoon ground black pepper

4 to 6 Amazing Flourless Hamburger Buns (page 89), toasted

1. In an electric pressure cooker, add—in this order—the red onion, lentils, bell pepper, stock, tomato sauce, Worcestershire, maple syrup, vinegar, paprika, chili powder, garlic powder, dried onion, sea salt, and black pepper. Do not stir.

2. Place the lid on the cooker and make sure the vent valve is in the SEALING position. Using the display panel, select the MANUAL/PRESSURE COOK function and HIGH PRESSURE, and use the +/− buttons until the display reads 15 minutes.

3. When the cooker beeps to let you know it's finished, let it naturally release pressure until the display reads LO:5. Switch the vent valve from the SEALING to the VENTING position. Use caution while the steam escapes—it's hot.

4. Stir well and serve the sloppy joe mixture sandwiched between the buns.

THE ULTIMATE VEGGIE BURGER WITH BASIL PESTO AIOLI

Okay. Make these. Please. They are really really good. I was skeptical at first, using portobello mushrooms to replace the meat in a burger? I won't make any claims like "this tastes exactly like meat" because it doesn't. It tastes like what it is—and what it is, is pretty dang delicious. It's also a very nice change of pace. Don't skimp on the sauce. That stuff is like manna from heaven.

—————————————————— SERVES 4 ——————————————————

¼ cup avocado oil

2 tablespoons balsamic vinegar

¼ teaspoon fine sea salt

⅛ teaspoon ground black pepper

4 small to medium portobello mushroom, wiped clean and stems removed

1 red bell pepper, seeded and cut into fourths

1 small red onion, sliced into ½-inch rounds

4 Amazing Flourless Hamburger Buns (page 89)

Basil Pesto Aioli (page 223)

1. In a small bowl, whisk together the oil, vinegar, sea salt, and black pepper.

2. Add the mushrooms to the air fryer basket. Top each with a piece of bell pepper and an onion round. Evenly drizzle the oil-vinegar mixture over the top of each veggie stack. Bake at 400°F for 15 minutes (see Note).

3. Carefully remove the veggie stacks with tongs, tilting them slightly to allow any excess liquid to drip off. Transfer to a plate and cover with foil.

4. To assemble, toast the buns, slather the aioli on both sides of each bun, and sandwich a veggie stack.

Note: If you do not have an air fryer, you can bake the veggie stacks in a conventional oven at 450°F for 22 to 24 minutes.

BASIL PESTO AIOLI

This sauce is absolutely fabulous. Use any leftovers in place of mayo on sandwiches, or make the Pesto-Aioli Tomato Pie (page 58)—it's awesome paired with tomatoes and corn!

MAKES 1 CUP

¾ cup avocado oil

1 large egg, at room temperature

8 medium fresh basil leaves

½ teaspoon dried minced onion

2 cloves garlic, roughly chopped

2 tablespoons pine nuts

2 tablespoons fresh lemon juice

½ teaspoon fine sea salt

Combine all ingredients in a wide-mouth mason jar and blend with an immersion blender on medium speed until smooth and creamy. Keeps in the refrigerator for up to 6 days.

VEGGIE SPRING ROLLS

If you've never made veggie spring rolls, you're a missing out on a really yummy lunch! This is a great starter recipe, because the sky is the limit when it comes to spring roll fillings: sesame sauce with basil and avocado, garlic chicken with cilantro and brown rice, or the coconut shrimp on page 196 with the sweet chili mint sauce. I get my wrappers in the Asian section at Walmart. The kind I buy have only five ingredients and are gluten-free and verified by the Non-GMO Project! Not only are they healthy, but they're low in calories and make an awesome vessel for sandwiches and wraps. Two to three rolls make a nice, light lunch if you think you might be having something heavier for dinner.

—————————— **MAKES 6 ROLLS** ——————————

½ cup chopped fresh cilantro stems and leaves

1 medium carrot, peeled and julienned

½ cup julienned seeded red bell pepper

½ cup julienned English cucumber

½ cup shredded purple cabbage

2 tablespoons fresh mint leaves

6 (10-inch diameter) brown-rice spring roll wrappers

½ head green leaf lettuce

4 ounces micro greens or bean sprouts

⅓ cup Spicy Peanut Sauce (page 226)

1. Place the cilantro, carrot, bell pepper, cucumber, cabbage, and mint in a medium bowl. Toss to combine and set aside.

2. Fill a pie pan or a large deep plate with warm water. Add one rice wrapper and soak for 20 seconds. Remove the wrapper and set on a textured surface such as a wood or plastic cutting board.

3. Place one or two lettuce leaves in the center of the wrapper, spoon one-sixth of the vegetable mixture on top, and then top with some of the micro greens. Fold the two sides of the paper inward and hold in place. Take the bottom side, fold over the filling, and tuck in. Roll upwards from the bottom to form a tight roll.

4. Repeat to make five more rolls. Serve with the peanut sauce for dipping.

SPICY PEANUT SAUCE

Spicy peanut sauce can be found at most stores, or you can skip the preservatives and make it at home! Really, this stuff is a breeze to whip up, and you won't have to worry about hidden MSG. If you're not a fan of heat, do not add the full tablespoon of sriracha; add it little by little until the sauce is adjusted to your preference. Serve a half-recipe with the spring rolls or any of your favorite Asian-inspired dishes, or use the full amount to make the Spicy Thai Pizza (page 232).

MAKES ⅔ CUP

¼ cup creamy organic peanut butter

¼ cup rice wine vinegar

1 tablespoon 100% pure maple syrup

2 tablespoons coconut aminos

1 to 2 tablespoons sriracha or red chili sauce

2 green onions, finely chopped

Combine all ingredients except the green onion in a wide-mouth mason jar and blend on high with an immersion blender. Stir in the green onion. Store covered in the refrigerator and use within 5 days.

CRISPY ORANGE CAULIFLOWER

This recipe, a play on the Chinese restaurant favorite Orange Chicken, makes my top-five favorites in this book. Last year, we went out for drinks with a couple of friends and there was vegan, crispy cauliflower on the menu. We decided to try it, not expecting much. HOLY COW! It straight blew my mind. The texture and taste were both just like chicken! I set out to recapture the magic we enjoyed at that bar at home and created this crispy orange cauliflower. I'm really proud of this recipe and hope you enjoy it too.

SERVES 4

FOR THE CAULIFLOWER

¾ cup gluten-free oat flour (see Note)

¼ teaspoon garlic powder

¼ teaspoon fine sea salt

2 large eggs or Flax Eggs (page 229)

1 large head cauliflower, cored and cut into bite-size florets

Avocado or coconut oil cooking spray

FOR THE ORANGE SAUCE

½ teaspoon grated orange zest

¼ cup fresh squeezed orange juice (mandarin orange juice works too) (see Note)

2 cloves garlic, minced

¼ teaspoon grated fresh ginger

1. For the cauliflower: Combine the oat flour, garlic powder, and sea salt in a bowl. In a separate bowl, whisk the eggs until light and frothy. One handful at a time, dip the cauliflower florets in the eggs, coating each piece well, then use your dry hand to dredge the florets in the oat flour mixture to coat. Once thoroughly coated, set the cauliflower inside a 5.3-quart air fryer basket. Repeat until you have one layer of cauliflower on the bottom of the basket, then spray the cauliflower with avocado oil. Continue to add layers until all of the cauliflower is coated and inside the basket.

2. Bake the cauliflower at 340°F for 15 minutes (see Note).

3. While the cauliflower bakes, make the sauce: Combine all the sauce ingredients in a saucepan over medium-high heat. Cook, whisking continuously, until the sauce begins to bubble and thicken. Check to see that the sauce is ready by dipping in a spoon: If the sauce coats the spoon without falling off immediately, it's ready. Set aside.

4. When the air fryer beeps to signal that it's finished, use a wooden spoon to stir the cauliflower, then bake for 10 minutes longer at 400°F, stopping to toss once halfway through.

continued on page 229

2 tablespoons rice wine
vinegar

2 tablespoons coconut aminos

2 teaspoons arrowroot flour

1 teaspoon sriracha

½ teaspoon sesame oil

5. Transfer the cauliflower to a large bowl. Drizzle with the orange sauce and toss with a spoon, making sure all the pieces are coated. Serve warm.

Note: If you have a high-powered blender, make your oat flour at home! Add ¾ cup gluten-free old-fashioned oats to the blender and blend on high for 20 seconds.

Note: If you do not have an air fryer, you can bake the cauliflower florets on a baking sheet in a conventional oven at 400°F for 25 to 30 minutes, flipping the florets halfway through.

Note: If your oranges aren't very sweet, add a tablespoon of 100% pure maple syrup to the sauce.

FLAX EGGS

A great egg replacer if you can't consume eggs! When you mix flax meal with water and let it sit, it becomes gelatinous and resembles the consistency of egg yolks. This is a great substitute in dishes that call for three eggs or less. Double the recipe as needed.

MAKES ENOUGH TO REPLACE 1 LARGE EGG

2½ tablespoons water

1 tablespoon ground flax meal

In a bowl, combine the water and flax meal, stir with a spoon, and let sit to thicken for 2 minutes.

SUMMER ZUCCHINI PASTA

Last summer, I brought this to several potlucks and it was always a hit! I was constantly asked for the recipe. It also makes a really filling lunch or dinner salad, and it's just flat-out pretty to look at. Plus, no cooking required!

SERVES 4 TO 6

½ cup avocado oil

Juice of 2 limes (about ¼ cup)

1 teaspoon ground cumin

1 teaspoon garlic powder

1 teaspoon fine sea salt

⅛ teaspoon cayenne pepper

2 medium to large zucchini, spiralized

5 ounces cherry tomatoes, halved

1 (15-ounce) can black beans, rinsed and drained

1 ripe medium avocado, pitted, peeled, and diced

½ medium red onion, diced

1 cup frozen corn, thawed

½ cup fresh cilantro stems and leaves, chopped

In a bowl, combine the avocado oil, lime juice, cumin, garlic powder, sea salt, and cayenne. In a second large bowl, combine the spiralized zucchini, cherry tomatoes, black beans, avocado, onion, corn, and cilantro. Add the dressing to the zucchini mixture, toss the ingredients to combine, and serve.

SPICY THAI PIZZA

Pizza Night happens frequently at our home. The gluten-free crust is easy to whip up and top with all of your favorite fixins. I usually enjoy a couple slices with a Simple House Salad (page 122). The extra serving of veggies helps me control my over-indulgent nature.

— SERVES 4 —

FOR THE DOUGH

⅔ cup cassava flour, plus more as needed for rolling

⅓ cup arrowroot flour

½ teaspoon onion powder

½ teaspoon garlic powder

1 teaspoon fine sea salt

1 large egg

⅓ cup water

2½ tablespoons extra-virgin olive oil

FOR THE PIZZA

⅔ cup Spicy Peanut Sauce (page 226, omitting the green onion)

1 cup shredded mozzarella cheese

1 medium carrot, peeled and shredded

⅓ cup thinly sliced snow peas

¼ cup thinly sliced yellow bell pepper

¼ cup chopped green onions

3 tablespoons chopped fresh cilantro leaves

1. Place a pizza stone or baking steel on the middle rack of the oven. Preheat the oven to 425°F.

2. For the dough: Combine the cassava flour, arrowroot flour, onion powder, garlic powder, and sea salt in a medium bowl. Add the egg, water, and olive oil and mix well. Shape the dough into a ball and let rest for 5 minutes. After resting, the ball should not be sticky; if it is, add a little more cassava flour.

3. Sprinkle a sheet of parchment paper with cassava flour. Flatten the dough with your hands and place another sheet of parchment paper on top. Use a rolling pin, gently roll the dough out to a thin 10-inch round; you're pressing and shaping with the rolling pin, more than actually rolling. This flour contains no gluten and is not stretchy, so working with the dough will be different than working with regular wheat flour dough.

4. Remove the top sheet of parchment paper. Take the pizza stone out of the oven and place the dough, still on the parchment, on top of the stone. Put the stone back in the oven and par-bake the crust for 5 minutes.

5. Remove the stone with the dough from the oven and use a spoon to spread ½ cup of the peanut sauce on the crust, then top with the mozzarella cheese. Put the stone back in the oven and bake for 5 to 7 minutes, until the edges of the crust have browned.

6. Remove the pizza from the oven and top with the carrot, snow peas, bell pepper, green onions, cilantro, and drizzle with remaining peanut sauce. Serve.

BUTTERNUT SQUASH CHIPOTLE CHILI

Embracing the Instant Loss lifestyle meant learning to love and embrace plant food. When I was younger, I struggled with consuming vegetable-based meals, so I want my kids to love how fueling their bodies with plant food makes them feel. To do this, I like to sneak as many vegan dishes as I can into our meal rotation. I try to get creative. Most of the time, no one even misses the meat! This delicious vegan chili is a regular fall favorite in our home. The chili pairs well with Golden Sweet Corn Bread (page 80).

SERVES 6

1 medium butternut squash (about 2 pounds), peeled and cut into 1-inch cubes

2 large beefsteak tomatoes, diced

1 medium red onion, finely chopped

1 medium red bell pepper, seeded and diced

3 cups black beans from cans, rinsed and drained

2 cups low-sodium or homemade vegetable stock

5 cloves garlic, minced

2 tablespoons extra-virgin olive oil

1 tablespoon chili powder

1 tablespoon chopped chipotle pepper in adobo sauce

1 teaspoon ground cumin

1 bay leaf

1 teaspoon fine sea salt (see Note)

¼ teaspoon ground black pepper

½ cup chopped fresh cilantro

1. Place all of the ingredients except the cilantro in an electric pressure cooker and stir to combine. Place the lid on the cooker and make sure the vent valve is in the SEALING position. Using the display panel, select the MANUAL/PRESSURE COOK function and HIGH PRESSURE, and use the +/− buttons until the display reads 10 minutes.

2. When the cooker beeps to let you know it's finished, switch the vent valve from the SEALING to the VENTING position, administering a quick release. Use caution while the steam escapes—it's hot. Remove the bay leaf, stir in the fresh cilantro, and serve warm.

Note: If you're using a homemade salt-free stock, you'll need to add ¼ to ½ teaspoon additional sea salt.

Note: The chili is a great freezer meal: Just place all the ingredients, except for the stock and cilantro, in a gallon-size freezer bag and store in the freezer until ready to make. On a busy night, simply dump the bag of ingredients inside the pressure cooker, add the stock, and cook according to the instructions (no need to add additional time).

sides

Veggie Brown Rice

Braised Cabbage with Bacon

Smoky Chipotle Refried Black Beans

Cheesy Oats

Garlic Mashed Cauliflower

Honey-Sriracha Brussels Sprouts

Lemon-Garlic Quinoa

Darn Good Green Beans

Cauliflower "Potato" Salad

Garlic-Balsamic Roasted Asparagus

Lemon-Roasted Broccoli with Pine Nuts and Pomegranate Seeds

VEGGIE BROWN RICE

This complex carb dish is a great source of plant energy. After an intense workout or if you're just craving something with a bit more "fill me up" power, this yummy rice is a quick side to serve alongside your favorite main course.

SERVES 6

2 cups vegetable broth (see page 109)

1½ cups long- or short-grain brown rice

2 cups frozen mixed vegetables (peas, carrots, corn, green beans)

2 tablespoons extra-virgin olive oil

Fine sea salt

Ground black pepper

1. Combine the vegetable broth and brown rice in an electric pressure cooker. Place the lid on the cooker and make sure the vent valve is in the SEALING position. Using the display panel, select the MULTIGRAIN function and HIGH PRESSURE (if your pot does not have this function, the MANUAL/PRESSURE COOK function can be used). Use the +/− buttons until the display reads 28 minutes.

2. When the cooker beeps to let you know it's finished, switch the vent valve from the SEALING to the VENTING position, administering a quick release. Use caution while the steam escapes—it's hot. Add the vegetables, olive oil, and sea salt and black pepper to taste and stir.

BRAISED CABBAGE WITH BACON

I love green cabbage, it's such a nutrient powerhouse! Full of vitamin K, it helps increase your concentration and mental function. It can even help dry up oily skin and acne! Packed full of savory flavor, this seemingly simple side just might be the star of the show.

SERVES 6

8 ounces nitrate-free bacon, diced

2 tablespoons salted butter or ghee

1 large head green cabbage, cored and cut into ¼-inch slices

1 large white onion, thinly sliced

1 medium Gala apple, cored and thinly sliced

2 tablespoons apple cider vinegar

½ teaspoon fine sea salt

¾ teaspoon ground black pepper

1. Preheat an electric pressure cooker using the SAUTÉ function. After pressing the SAUTÉ button, press the ADJUST button until MORE is highlighted. When the display panel reads HOT, add the bacon and butter and cook, stirring, until the bacon is crispy, about 10 minutes. Use a slotted spoon to transfer the bacon bits to a paper towel, leaving all that delicious fat in the pot.

2. Add the cabbage, onion, apple, apple cider vinegar, sea salt, and black pepper to the cooker and stir. Place the lid on the pressure cooker and make sure the vent valve is in the SEALING position. Using the display panel, press the CANCEL button and select the MANUAL/PRESSURE COOK function and HIGH PRESSURE. Use the +/− buttons until the display reads 10.

3. When the cooker beeps to let you know it's finished, switch the vent valve from the SEALING to the VENTING position, administering a quick release. Use caution while the steam escapes—it's hot.

4. Add the bacon to the cabbage and stir. Serve warm.

SMOKY CHIPOTLE REFRIED BLACK BEANS

This is a cost-effective filler. Because my kids are growing, feeding them a quality meat protein with every meal can be pricey. To help make it less so, we fill the gap with beans and legumes. These beans are perfect to serve as a side on Taco Night, and nice to keep in the refrigerator for a quick burrito lunch. I'll make burritos with organic tortillas for the kiddos and assemble a burrito bowl for myself. It's really simple, just skip the tortilla and put all the innards in a bowl.

SERVES 6 TO 8

8 ounces dried black beans

5½ cups water

1 yellow onion, diced

¼ cup bacon grease

¼ cup fresh cilantro stems and leaves, chopped

1 tablespoon ground cumin

1 teaspoon chipotle chili powder

½ teaspoon garlic powder

½ teaspoon fine sea salt

¼ teaspoon cayenne pepper

1. In a bowl, soak the black beans in 4 cups of water for 8 hours or overnight. Rinse and drain.

2. In an electric pressure cooker, combine the black beans with 1½ cups water and the remaining ingredients. Stir.

3. Place the lid on the cooker and make sure the vent valve is in the SEALING position. Using the display panel, select the MANUAL/PRESSURE COOK function and HIGH PRESSURE, and use the +/− buttons until the display reads 18 minutes.

4. When the cooker beeps to let you know it's finished, let it naturally release pressure until the display reads LO:10. Switch the vent valve from the SEALING to the VENTING position. Use caution while the steam escapes—it's hot.

5. Use an immersion blender on high speed to puree the beans, or a potato masher for a chunkier refried bean.

CHEESY OATS

Love cheese grits? Me too! These cheesy oats are for us! Savory and oh so very cheesy, they are also heart healthy! Because of their low glycemic index, they can help regulate your blood sugar and lower your cholesterol. This is a nutrient rich, gluten-free, whole grain side dish that feels naughty but is just flat-out GOOD!

SERVES 4

2½ cups water

⅓ cup chopped peeled carrot

¼ cup unfortified nutritional yeast

¼ cup arrowroot flour

1 tablespoon salted butter or ghee

1 teaspoon fine sea salt

1 cup gluten-free old-fashioned rolled oats

1. Place 1½ cups water, the carrot, nutritional yeast, arrowroot flour, butter, and sea salt in a high-powered blender and blend on high until combined. The mixture will be watery. Add the blender contents to a 6-cup baking dish that fits inside your electric pressure cooker, stir in the oats, and cover with foil.

2. Add 1 cup water to the pressure cooker. Place the trivet inside the cooker and add the baking dish.

3. Place the lid on the cooker and make sure the vent valve is in the SEALING position. Using the display panel, select the MANUAL/PRESSURE COOK function and HIGH PRESSURE, and use the +/− buttons until the display reads 10 minutes.

4. When the cooker beeps to let you know it's finished, switch the vent valve from the SEALING to the VENTING position, administering a quick release. Open the cooker and lift the oats out. Remove the foil and stir the oats. This is best served immediately.

GARLIC MASHED CAULIFLOWER

I rebelled against the idea of using cauliflower as a substitute for mashed potatoes for a very long time. I guess I needed to heed that classic advice: "Don't knock it 'til you've tried it." This simple cauliflower mash is a pretty adequate substitute for mashed spuds if you're trying to keep your starchy vegetables at a minimum. Try it with the Sirloin Steak Strips with Mushrooms and Balsamic Glaze (page 173)—so good!

SERVES 2 TO 4

1 cup water

1 large head cauliflower, cored and cut into large florets

1 teaspoon fine sea salt

½ teaspoon garlic powder

1. Add 1 cup water to an electric pressure cooker. Place a trivet or steamer basket inside. Put the cauliflower on the trivet. Place the lid on the cooker and make sure the vent valve is in the SEALING position. Using the display panel, select the MANUAL/PRESSURE COOK function and HIGH PRESSURE, and use the +/− buttons until the display reads 3 minutes.

2. When the cooker beeps to let you know it's finished, switch the vent valve from the SEALING to the VENTING position, administering a quick release. Use caution while the steam escapes—it's hot.

3. Open the cooker, remove and drain the cauliflower, then place in a medium bowl. Stir in the sea salt and garlic powder. Using an emersion blender, blend until smooth. Serve warm.

HONEY-SRIRACHA BRUSSELS SPROUTS

With just the right amount of heat, these Brussels sprouts are so good you'll be tempted to eat the whole pan! I love to pair them with Blackened Salmon (page 183). They also keep well in the fridge. Make a pot on Sunday and portion them for lunches throughout the week!

SERVES 4 TO 6

1 tablespoon salted butter or ghee

½ medium yellow onion, thinly sliced

1 pound Brussels sprouts, trimmed

¼ cup raw honey

1 tablespoon sriracha

½ teaspoon fine sea salt

1½ teaspoons arrowroot flour

1. Preheat an electric pressure cooker using the SAUTÉ function. After pressing the SAUTÉ button, press the ADJUST button until MORE is highlighted. When the display panel reads HOT, add the butter and onion and cook, stirring, until the onion becomes fragrant and translucent, about 3 minutes. Add the Brussels sprouts and toss with the onion. In a bowl, combine the honey and sriracha, then drizzle over the Brussels sprouts. Add the sea salt and stir to combine.

2. Place the lid on the cooker and make sure the vent valve is in the SEALING position. Using the display panel, select the STEAM function and HIGH PRESSURE, and use the +/− buttons until the display reads 2 minutes.

3. When the cooker beeps to let you know it's finished, switch the vent valve from the SEALING to the VENTING position, administering a quick release. Use caution while the steam escapes—it's hot.

4. Open the lid, add the arrowroot flour, and stir to combine. The Instant Pot will automatically keep the dish warm after cooking is complete. The longer the Brussels sprouts sit in the honey-sriracha after cooking, the better they taste. Serve warm.

LEMON-GARLIC QUINOA

This quinoa pairs beautifully with chicken or fish, but I also love to add it to salad. Light and fresh, it's a great summertime side. The fluffy texture and a hit of lemon juice really complement the slight garlic flavor.

SERVES 4

1½ cups water

1 cup quinoa, rinsed and drained

¼ cup fresh lemon juice

½ teaspoon garlic powder

¼ teaspoon fine sea salt

1 cup chopped baby spinach

1. In an electric pressure cooker, combine the water, quinoa, lemon juice, garlic powder, and sea salt and stir.

2. Place the lid on the cooker and make sure the vent valve is in the SEALING position. Using the display panel, select the MANUAL/PRESSURE COOK function and HIGH PRESSURE, and use the +/− buttons until the display reads 1 minute.

3. When the cooker beeps to let you know it's finished, let it naturally release the pressure until the display reads LO:10. Switch the vent valve from the SEALING to the VENTING position. Use caution while the steam escapes—it's hot. Open the lid and stir in the baby spinach. Once the spinach has wilted, fluff the quinoa with a fork and serve.

DARN GOOD GREEN BEANS

These green beans are packed full of Mediterranean flavor and they're just so darn good! I make a large batch and store them inside an airtight container in the refrigerator to reheat them with lunch throughout the week! P.S. You can add bacon, if you're into that kind of thing . . .

SERVES 6

---

2 pounds fresh green beans, ends trimmed

½ cup vegetable broth (see page 109)

½ cup freshly grated Parmesan cheese

5 cloves garlic, minced

1 tablespoon extra-virgin olive oil

1½ teaspoons balsamic vinegar

2 teaspoons dried basil

Fine sea salt

1. Combine all of the ingredients in an electric pressure cooker. Place the lid on the cooker and make sure the vent valve is in the SEALING position. Using the display panel, select the MANUAL/PRESSURE COOK function and LOW PRESSURE, and use the +/– buttons until the display reads 5 minutes.

2. When the cooker beeps to let you know it's finished, switch the vent valve from the SEALING to the VENTING position, administering a quick release. Use caution while the steam escapes—it's hot.

3. Add salt to taste and serve warm.

CAULIFLOWER "POTATO" SALAD

What an excellent potluck dish! Anytime we go to a friend or family member's house for a meal, I always offer to bring two things: a dessert and a side dish. That way, no matter where I am, I always know I have at least two things I can eat! This potato salad-esque dish is the perfect side for a cookout!

SERVES 6
---

1 cup water

1 large head cauliflower, cored and cut into large florets

1 cup finely chopped celery

⅓ cup finely chopped red onion

½ cup Homemade Mayo (page 264) or store-bought mayonnaise

1 tablespoon yellow mustard

1½ teaspoons apple cider vinegar

¼ teaspoon garlic powder

½ teaspoon fine sea salt

¼ teaspoon ground black pepper

1. Add 1 cup water to an electric pressure cooker. Place a steamer basket inside and fill with the cauliflower florets.

2. Place the lid on the cooker and make sure the vent valve is in the SEALING position. Using the display panel, select the STEAM function and HIGH PRESSURE, and use the +/− buttons until the display reads 1 minute.

3. When the cooker beeps to let you know it's finished, switch the vent valve from the SEALING to the VENTING position, administering a quick release. Use caution while the steam escapes—it's hot.

4. Open the cooker, remove and drain the cauliflower, then transfer to a large bowl to let cool. Cut the cauliflower into bite-size pieces and return to the bowl.

5. Add the celery, onion, mayo, mustard, apple cider vinegar, garlic powder, sea salt, and black pepper to the cauliflower. Mix well with a spoon to combine, then refrigerate until chilled, or up to 3 days. Serve chilled.

GARLIC-BALSAMIC ROASTED ASPARAGUS

Just like candy, I have to be very careful while eating these spears or, before I know it, they're all gone. This is a simple garlic and balsamic asparagus, but you can mix it up with your favorite seasonings to suit your tastes. Add Parmesan for richer flavor, omit the balsamic vinegar and dust with a bit of taco seasoning for a Mexican flair, or keep it simple with sea salt, black pepper, and olive oil. You can't go wrong!

SERVES 2

1 bunch asparagus, woody ends removed

1½ teaspoons extra-virgin olive oil

1½ teaspoons balsamic vinegar

½ teaspoon garlic powder

¼ teaspoon fine sea salt

1. In a large bowl, toss the asparagus with the olive oil, balsamic vinegar, garlic powder, and sea salt.

2. Add the asparagus to the basket of a 5.3-quart air fryer and bake at 380°F for 5 minutes (see Note). Shake the basket to toss the asparagus and bake for 2 minutes longer. Serve warm.

Note: If you do not have an air fryer, you can bake the asparagus on a baking sheet in a conventional oven at 425°F for 12 to 15 minutes depending on the thickness of the asparagus.

LEMON-ROASTED BROCCOLI WITH PINE NUTS AND POMEGRANATE SEEDS

I used to make this on a sheet pan but it cooks up much quicker in my air fryer! No need to wait for the oven to preheat. Just throw everything in the basket and in 12 minutes, you have perfectly roasted broccoli.

SERVES 2

---

1 pound broccoli florets, cut into bite-size pieces

2 tablespoons raw pine nuts

1 tablespoon extra-virgin olive oil

1 tablespoon fresh lemon juice

½ teaspoon garlic powder

¼ teaspoon fine sea salt

⅛ teaspoon ground black pepper

2 tablespoons pomegranate seeds

1. In a large bowl, combine the broccoli, pine nuts, olive oil, lemon juice, garlic powder, sea salt, and black pepper. Stir to combine, making sure all of the broccoli is coated.

2. Add the broccoli and pine nuts to the basket of a 5.3-quart air fryer and bake at 350°F for 12 minutes, stirring every 5 minutes (see Note). Transfer to a large bowl, stir in pomegranate seeds, and serve immediately.

Note: If you don't have an air fryer, you can roast the broccoli on a baking sheet in a 400°F oven for 30 minutes, tossing halfway through.

green goddess dressing

blueberry jam

easy three-ingredient homemade tahini

tangy barbecue
sauce

best
guacamole
ever

dressings and sauces

Ranch Dressing

Green Goddess Dressing

Homemade Mayo

Blueberry Jam

Hemp Milk

Easy Three-Ingredient Homemade Tahini

Tangy Barbecue Sauce

Best Guacamole Ever

RANCH DRESSING

I don't know if it's a Southern thing, but I could just about put ranch dressing on anything and everything. I used to be a Hidden Valley girl, and for months my Aunt Kim was telling me that I should make my own. Why make it when you can buy a packet of Hidden Valley and mix it with buttermilk, right?

Well, let me tell you why. Packets, like the one just mentioned, are usually full of sugar, tons of sodium, flavor enhancers, and preservatives. I quit my Hidden Valley habit and I started making my own, so now I can have ranch without the heaping pile of guilt.

Make sure to find a sour cream that is only cultured cream, I use Daisy brand.

MAKES 1 HEAPING CUP

1 large egg, at room temperature

¾ cup avocado oil

¼ cup sour cream

1 teaspoon apple cider vinegar

1 teaspoon dried parsley

1 teaspoon garlic powder

1 teaspoon dried minced onion

⅛ teaspoon dry mustard

½ teaspoon fine sea salt

Combine all of the ingredients in a wide-mouth mason jar. Blend with an immersion blender on medium speed until smooth and creamy. Place the lid on the jar and store in the refrigerator for up to 6 days.

GREEN GODDESS DRESSING

This delightful, everyday salad dressing is best fresh, but keeps for 3 to 4 days in the refrigerator. It's full of healthy fats and ingredients that you probably have in your pantry right now! It's also delightful on turkey sandwiches, inside lettuce wraps, or tossed with your favorite salad.

MAKES ½ CUP

½ ripe medium avocado, pitted, peeled, and diced

¼ cup water

1 green onion, finely chopped

1 tablespoon fresh flat-leaf parsley leaves

1 tablespoon avocado oil

1 teaspoon apple cider vinegar

1 teaspoon lemon juice

¼ teaspoon garlic powder

¼ teaspoon fine sea salt

Combine all the ingredients in a wide-mouth mason jar. Blend on high with an immersion blender. Store in the refrigerator and use within 5 days.

HOMEMADE MAYO

I put off making my own mayo for years, it just sounded too difficult. But really, it's one of the quickest things to whip up. Just add everything to a jar and blend. You want to make sure to use an immersion blender, though. It won't work with simple whisking. You can also use a blender with variable speeds, but there is more chance for error as it's a little more tricky to get right. A blender or a food processor doesn't give you quite as much control over the speed.

Mayonnaise can be a little temperamental, so you want to ensure that all of your ingredients are at room temperature and that you keep the immersion blender blade submerged completely. Do that and you'll be just fine! Once you get it right, you'll never use store-bought mayo again!

— MAKES 1 CUP —

1 large egg, at room temperature (see Note)

1 cup avocado oil

¼ teaspoon dried ground mustard

¼ teaspoon red wine vinegar

¼ teaspoon fine sea salt

Combine all ingredients in a wide-mouth mason jar and blend on high with an immersion blender. As you blend, very slowly raise the blender up through the mixture, keeping it submerged. Once the mayo has partially emulsified, you may have to move the blender up and down to blend any remaining oil. Store the mayo in the refrigerator for up to 6 days.

Note: Eggs can be run under warm water to reach room temperature more quickly. Keep homemade mayo for no longer than 1 week due to the presence of the raw eggs.

BLUEBERRY JAM

Finding a quality store-bought jam without boatloads of artificial sweetener or sugar can be a challenge. That's why we like to make our own. In addition to blueberry jam, you can make any number of other berry jams with this same method. Have fun and experiment with different fruits and flavors!

MAKES ¼ CUP

2 cups blueberries, fresh or frozen

¼ cup raw honey

¼ teaspoon ground cinnamon

¼ teaspoon ground nutmeg

1. In a saucepan, combine all the ingredients. Cook over medium-high heat, whisking, until the blueberries break down, about 5 minutes. Lower the heat to a simmer and whisk occasionally until the mixture thickens, about 15 minutes.

2. Remove from the heat and let cool. Store covered in the refrigerator and use within 1 week.

HEMP MILK

Can't have almonds? Tired of the overpowering coconut flavor that coconut milk can leave in dishes? Hemp milk is a great alternative. Hemp hearts are a protein-packed plant food that add a great crunch to smoothie bowls, oatmeal, and salads. But did you know they also make a fabulous milk?

MAKES 1 QUART

3 cups water

½ cup hemp hearts

1½ teaspoons 100% pure maple syrup

⅛ teaspoon fine sea salt

1. Combine all of the ingredients in a high-powered blender. Blend on high until there are no remaining pieces of hemp hearts, 1 to 2 minutes.

2. Strain the hemp milk through a nut milk bag or piece of cheesecloth, wringing well (see Note). Store the hemp milk in a glass container in the refrigerator and use within 5 to 7 days.

Note: Compost the leftover hemp pulp or use it for an extra protein boost in your morning smoothies!

EASY THREE-INGREDIENT HOMEMADE TAHINI

Tahini, a nut-free butter alternative, is a delicious sesame seed butter that has a mild flavor and is great for use in recipes like Snickerdoodles (page 305) and hummus! You can also add a little bit of your favorite sweetener and enjoy it on Gluten-Free English Muffin Thins (page 77). It can also be used in any recipe that calls for peanut or almond butter.

MAKES 1 CUP

2 cups raw sesame seeds

5 tablespoons extra-virgin olive oil, plus a little extra (if needed)

¼ teaspoon fine sea salt

1. Heat a cast-iron skillet over medium heat. Add the sesame seeds to the skillet and toast until they have a nice golden color, 2 to 3 minutes. Use a wooden spoon to keep them circulating in the pan so they don't burn.

2. Transfer the seeds to a small food processor or blender. Add the oil and sea salt and blend on high until smooth and creamy, about 2 minutes. If your tahini is thicker than the consistency of peanut butter, add a little more oil to thin it. If you have a wide base blender or a large food processor, you'll want to double the recipe so that nothing gets trapped beneath the blades. Cover the tahini and store in the refrigerator for up to 2 months.

TANGY BARBECUE SAUCE

Our family absolutely loves barbecue sauce, but unfortunately, most of the sauces sold in stores have artificial colors and highly refined sugars. No problem though, because barbecue sauce is easy to make at home—it comes together in no time at all. Even better, it's made from ingredients you probably have in your pantry right now! To be more efficient, I recommend making a big batch and freezing the sauce in muffin trays. After the sauce has frozen, transfer it to freezer-safe bags and store for up to 4 months. This way, you'll have small portions on hand whenever needed.

MAKES 2½ CUPS

1 (15-ounce) can tomato sauce

2 tablespoons coconut sugar

2 tablespoons raw honey

1 tablespoon apple cider vinegar

1½ teaspoons reduced-sodium Worcestershire sauce

1½ teaspoons Dijon mustard

1 clove garlic, minced

½ teaspoon dried oregano

½ teaspoon chili powder

½ teaspoon ground black pepper

Combine all the ingredients in a high-powered blender that has the ability to heat its contents through blending (see Note). Blend on high for 5 minutes. You'll see the sauce thicken and steam and begin to come out of the top. Store in a glass jar in the fridge for up to 6 days.

Note: If you do not have a high-powered blender you can make the sauce on the stovetop: Bring all of the ingredients to a boil in a saucepan over medium-high heat. Lower to a simmer and cook, whisking occasionally so nothing burns on the bottom, for 5 minutes. Remove from the heat and let cool to room temperature before placing in a glass jar.

BEST GUACAMOLE EVER

I've been making this guac since before I started my health journey. It's rich in flavor and packed full of delicious whole foods. Just because you're eating well doesn't mean you need to sacrifice flavor. I'm asked to bring it to almost every family gathering, I have to triple or quadruple the recipe, and it's almost always the first thing gone. So when I say it's the best guacamole ever, I mean it!

MAKES 2 CUPS

3 ripe medium-large avocados, pitted and peeled

1 lime, juiced

½ teaspoon ground cumin

½ teaspoon fine sea salt

½ teaspoon cayenne pepper

½ yellow onion, diced

1 large Roma tomato, cored and diced

1 jalapeño, finely diced

2 tablespoons finely chopped fresh cilantro leaves and stems

1. In a large bowl, toss the avocados in the lime juice. Add the cumin, sea salt, and cayenne and mash with a potato masher to your desired consistency.

2. Fold in the onion, tomato, jalapeño, and cilantro. Serve immediately. Or cover with plastic wrap and store in the refrigerator for up to 24 hours.

snacks

Super Simple Granola

Party Nuts, Three Ways

Air Fryer Tortilla Chips with
Restaurant-Style Salsa

Four-Ingredient Corn Tortillas

White Bean Hummus

Kale Chips

Grain-Free Granola Bars

SUPER SIMPLE GRANOLA

Have you priced granola at the grocery store lately? It's crazy expensive. I gave that stuff up a long time ago, and now make mine at home. Y'all, it is so dang easy! We like to sprinkle granola over oatmeal for a nice little crunch or dairy-free ice cream for a tasty treat, or stir into dairy-free yogurt with some berries. With this staple in the pantry, the sky really is the limit!

——————————————— **MAKES 5 CUPS** ———————————————

3 cups gluten-free old-fashioned rolled oats

1 cup slivered almonds

¾ cup shredded unsweetened coconut flakes

¼ cup 100% pure maple syrup

¼ cup creamy peanut butter, almond butter, or tahini

¼ cup avocado oil

¾ teaspoon fine sea salt

1. Preheat the oven to 350°F. Line a baking sheet with parchment paper.

2. Combine all the ingredients in a large bowl, stir, and make sure everything is evenly coated. Spread the mixture on the prepared baking sheet and bake for 18 to 20 minutes, until the granola is golden and crisp.

3. Let the granola cool completely. Store in an airtight container in the pantry and use within 1 month.

PARTY NUTS, THREE WAYS

I have nothing against raw nuts, but does anybody else think they taste like tree bark? I don't eat them raw anymore (except in salads). Instead I got creative and flavor them with delicious seasonings and then roast in the air fryer. Take your pick from three of my favorite nut recipes. Or make all three and combine for a delicious nut medley.

CANDIED PARTY NUTS

MAKES 3 CUPS

1 cup raw walnuts

1 cup raw pecan halves

1 cup raw almonds

¼ cup 100% pure maple syrup

1 tablespoon melted salted butter or ghee

¼ teaspoon cayenne pepper

1 teaspoon fine sea salt

½ teaspoon ground black pepper

CHEDDAR-RANCH PARTY NUTS

MAKES 3 CUPS

1 cup raw walnuts

1 cup raw pecan halves

1 cup raw almonds

1 tablespoon melted salted butter or ghee

1 teaspoon unfortified nutritional yeast

1 teaspoon dried parsley

½ teaspoon garlic powder

½ teaspoon onion powder

¾ teaspoon fine sea salt

SPICY BUFFALO ALMONDS

1 cup raw almonds

1 tablespoon Frank's RedHot sauce

1½ teaspoons melted salted butter or ghee

1 teaspoon red wine vinegar

¼ teaspoon garlic powder

⅛ teaspoon fine sea salt

1. Chose which variety of nuts to make from the lists above and combine all the ingredients in a large bowl. Stir with a spoon to combine. Transfer the nuts to a 5.3-quart air fryer basket and bake at 350°F for 7 minutes, opening the air fryer to stir the nuts halfway through (see Note).

2. Carefully remove the nuts from the air fryer and lay flat on a baking sheet or a large plate to cool completely, about 15 minutes. The nuts taste the best after sitting for about 8 hours, but can be consumed 15 minutes after baking. Once cooled, store in an airtight container at room temp for up to 10 days.

Note: If you do not have an air fryer, bake the coated nuts in a conventional oven on a baking sheet lined with parchment paper. Bake at 350°F for 14 to 16 minutes, flipping the nuts halfway through.

AIR FRYER TORTILLA CHIPS WITH RESTAURANT-STYLE SALSA

Who doesn't love to have a small evening snack while watching television? Before 8 p.m., I'll have my after-dinner indulgence. Sometimes it's a sweet, but usually it's something savory, like these chips and salsa. I try to drag it out and make the chips last over a 30-minute TV show, savoring every bite. Chips and salsa are my thing, but this also helps me keep from overeating. Don't be weirded out by the carrot in the salsa. That was Brady's brainchild—it contributes a bit of sweetness without adding sugar!

MAKES 2 CUPS SALSA AND 4 CUPS CHIPS

FOR THE RESTAURANT-STYLE SALSA

1 large carrot, peeled and chopped

1 cup fresh cilantro stems and leaves, chopped

½ cup drained pickled jalapeños, plus ½ cup of their juice

¼ cup tomato paste

6 cloves garlic, peeled

FOR THE TORTILLAS

10 corn tortillas, cut into sixths (see page 281, or use store-bought)

1 tablespoon avocado oil

½ teaspoon fine sea salt

1. For the salsa: Combine all the ingredients in a food processor and process until a blended salsa forms, about 30 seconds. Spoon the salsa into a container and refrigerate while you bake the tortilla chips.

2. For the tortillas: In large bowl, combine the tortillas, avocado oil, and sea salt. Toss until the tortillas are evenly coated. Place the tortillas in a 5.3-quart air fryer basket and bake at 350°F for 10 to 12 minutes, stirring every 3 minutes, until the tortillas firm up and turn golden brown (see Note). Transfer with tongs to a bowl. Serve with the salsa (see Note).

Note: If you do not have an air fryer, simply warm a large pan over medium-high heat on your stove top. Once the pan has warmed, add three tablespoons of oil to coat the bottom of the pan. Wait until the oil is hot. (You can test this by dropping a couple drops of water into the pan. If they sizzle the oil is ready.)

continued on page 278

Add as many tortilla triangles to the pan as will fit. Cook until golden on one side, about 2 minutes, then flip and cook the other side. The second side cooks much faster, sometimes in under 1 minute, so keep an eye on them.

When both sides of the tortilla chips are golden, remove them from the pan and lay them out to dry and cool on a paper towel. Lightly salt. Repeat this process until all of the tortillas are done.

Note: Store the salsa in a glass jar in the refrigerator for up to 5 days. You can also freeze it in an airtight freezer-safe container for up to 4 months. Store the chips in an airtight container at room temperature and consume within 3 days.

THREE-INGREDIENT CORN TORTILLAS

Everyone always asks me where I buy my corn tortillas. 99% of the time, we make them ourselves. First, they're extremely easy to make (especially with a tortilla press). Second, they literally have only three ingredients. That's all. Store-bought tortillas can have upwards of 20 different ingredients in order to keep them shelf stable.

If you are going to buy rather than make, I suggest looking for them at a health food store. Read the ingredient list. You should only see corn, salt, water, oil, and maybe some lime. You also want to make sure it's GMO-free corn. As always though, do the best you can, when you can! If you don't have any of these options, just buy what is available to you.

MAKES 12 (6-INCH) TORTILLAS

2 cups masa harina

1½ cups water

⅓ cup avocado oil

½ teaspoon fine sea salt

Note: Be sure to use the same side of the parchment paper for each tortilla, it will make the process much easier. Also note that you may have to use more than two pieces of paper, as they can tear easily once wet.

1. In a medium bowl, combine the masa harina, water, oil, and salt. Mix together well with a spoon or your hands until the mixture forms a dough. It should feel similar to a very soft Play-Doh; if the dough feels too dry, add more water, 1 tablespoon at a time. Divide the dough into 12 equal size balls.

2. Preheat an electric griddle to 350°F.

3. Cut two pieces of parchment paper, each 14 inches wide. Cover a large cutting board with one piece of paper. Place one ball on the paper and cover with the other piece of paper. Using a rolling pin or tortilla press, flatten the ball into an approximate 6-inch round about ⅛ inch thick.

4. Remove the top piece of paper. Lift the tortilla and bottom piece of paper together and flip both over onto the hot griddle. Slowly peel the paper from the tortilla and save to use with the next tortilla (see Note). Cook the tortilla until bubbles start to form inside, about 2 minutes. Using a spatula, flip and cook the second side for 1 to 2 minutes. Transfer the cooked tortilla to a plate and cover with foil to keep warm.

5. Repeat with the remaining dough balls to make 12 tortillas. Cover cooked tortillas in plastic wrap and they will keep in the refrigerator for up to three days.

WHITE BEAN HUMMUS

Hummus is an excellent and versatile snack and also one of my favorites! I love to pair it with fresh English cucumbers so I get that crunch that a chip usually lends. It's also a great salad topper and makes a fabulous sandwich spread.

MAKES 1¼ CUPS

1 (15-ounce) can white beans, rinsed and drained

¼ cup pine nuts

¼ cup extra-virgin olive oil or avocado oil

1½ teaspoons lemon juice

1 teaspoon garlic powder

½ teaspoon fine sea salt

Combine all the ingredients in a high-powered blender or a food processor. Blend on high until there are no remaining chunks and everything is smooth and creamy. Store in an airtight container inside the refrigerator for up to 6 days.

KALE CHIPS

Kale is so underused, but the health benefits are immense! Full of powerful antioxidants, a great source of fiber, high in calcium, vitamin K, vitamin C, and chlorophyll, this is a plant food we would all do well to eat more often! I usually include kale in smoothies but then forget to use it elsewhere. But why not make it the star and dehydrate it! These crunchy little kale chips are a powerhouse snack.

--- **SERVES 2** ---

1 bunch Tuscan kale, stems and ribs removed, leaves cut into 1-inch pieces

1 tablespoon extra-virgin olive oil

⅛ teaspoon fine sea salt

In a medium bowl, toss the kale leaves with the olive oil and sea salt. Place inside a 5.3-quart air fryer basket (see Note). Bake for 7 minutes at 390°F, stirring halfway through, until the chips are crispy, but not brown. Consume immediately or store at room temperature in an airtight container for up to 2 days.

Note: If you do not have an air fryer, bake the coated kale in a conventional oven at 350°F for 10 to 15 minutes, stirring halfway through.

GRAIN-FREE GRANOLA BARS

Great on the go, these bars full of nuts and seeds are designed to give you energy. They're great for a quick breakfast or an afternoon pick-me-up snack.

──────────── **MAKES 8 BARS** ────────────

¾ cup raw almonds, roughly chopped

½ cup raw walnuts, roughly chopped

⅓ cup unsweetened shredded coconut

2 tablespoons raw pumpkin seeds

2 tablespoons raw sunflower seeds

2 tablespoons raw hemp seeds

3 tablespoons 100% pure maple syrup

1 tablespoon extra-virgin coconut oil

1 teaspoon pure vanilla extract

½ teaspoon ground cinnamon

¼ teaspoon fine sea salt

1. In a dry skillet over medium heat, combine the almonds, walnuts, coconut, pumpkin seeds, sunflower seeds, and hemp seeds. Cook, stirring occasionally, for about 3 minutes, until the nuts begin to toast and become fragrant, being careful not to burn the coconut.

2. In a small saucepan over medium-high heat, combine maple syrup, coconut oil, vanilla, cinnamon, and sea salt. Stir and let simmer until it begins to thicken slightly, 2 to 3 minutes.

3. Pour the syrup into the nut and seed mixture and mix until coated.

4. Place a piece of parchment paper in the bottom of an 8×8-inch baking dish. With a wooden spoon or spatula, press the granola mixture evenly into the pan. Refrigerate for 1 hour.

5. Cut into eight bars. Wrap individually and place in an airtight container. Wrap individually and keep refrigerated for up to 2 weeks.

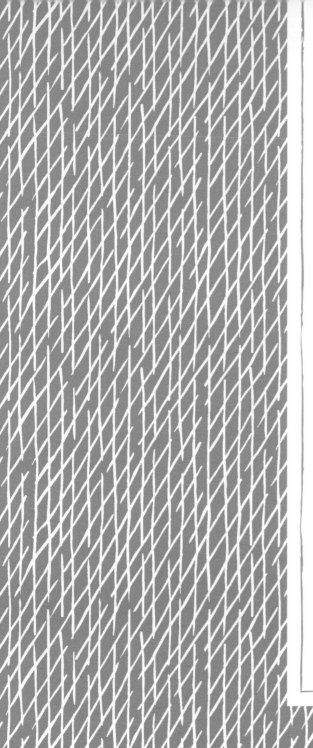

dessert

- Double-Chocolate Mocha Brownies
- Peach-Blueberry Cobbler
- Chewy Chocolate Chip Cookies
- Strawberry Shortcake Minis
- Strawberry-Coconut Mousse
- The Perfect Pumpkin Pie
- Snickerdoodles
- Maple Pecan Pie
- Buckeyes
- Jam Thumbprint Cookies
- Cookie Dough Pops
- Caramel Popcorn

DOUBLE-CHOCOLATE MOCHA BROWNIES

Decadent and so delicious, these grain-free brownies are something you'll want to write home about. The batter doesn't smell all that great because of the garbanzo bean flour, but the finished brownies are incredible! To all you bowl lickers out there, I don't recommend eating any of the batter, as the coffee granules need to be cooked in order to mellow everything out. If you do not have an air fryer, you can bake these in a conventional oven at 350°F for 22 to 25 minutes.

MAKES 6 BROWNIES

2 large eggs

½ cup garbanzo bean flour

½ cup coconut sugar

⅓ cup plus ¼ cup dairy-free chocolate chips

4 tablespoons salted butter or ghee, plus more for greasing the pan

2 tablespoons instant coffee or instant espresso granules

½ teaspoon vanilla

¼ teaspoon fine sea salt

1. Combine the eggs, garbanzo bean flour, coconut sugar, ⅓ cup of the chocolate chips, the butter, instant coffee, vanilla, and sea salt in a high-powered blender and blend on high for 1 minute. Stir in the remaining ¼ cup chocolate chips.

2. Grease a 6-cup baking dish. Using a spatula, scrape all the batter from the blender into the pan.

3. Place the pan inside the basket of a 5.3-quart air fryer and bake for 25 minutes at 350°F. The brownie is cooked through when it begins to pull away from the edge of the pan. Let cool inside the pan for 5 minutes before cutting the brownies. Serve warm or, once cool, store inside an airtight container at room temperature for up to 3 days.

PEACH-BLUEBERRY COBBLER

If you think this cobbler is delicious warm, try it the next morning right out of the fridge with a dollop of coconut whipped cream. I think my eyes just rolled back into my head from delight just thinking about it. I can hear the hallelujah chorus.

— SERVES 8 —

1½ pounds frozen peaches, thawed and thinly sliced (about 3 cups)

1 cup blueberries

½ cup plus 2 tablespoons coconut sugar

1½ tablespoons freshly grated lemon zest

1 tablespoon fresh lemon juice

½ cup plus 1 tablespoon cassava flour

1 cup gluten-free old-fashioned rolled oats

¼ cup softened salted butter or ghee

2 tablespoons water

½ teaspoon fine sea salt

Dairy-free ice cream or Coconut Whipped Cream (page 294)

1. Place the peaches, blueberries, 2 tablespoons of the coconut sugar, the lemon zest and juice, and 1 tablespoon of the cassava flour in a large bowl and stir to combine. Transfer to a 6-cup baking dish that fits inside your electric pressure cooker.

2. Combine the remaining ½ cup coconut sugar, remaining ½ cup cassava flour, the oats, butter, 2 tablespoons water, and salt in a food processor and pulse about 15 times to combine. Sprinkle the topping over the fruit evenly. Cover the dish with foil.

3. Add 1 cup water to the pressure cooker. Place the trivet in the cooker and add the baking dish.

4. Place the lid on the cooker and make sure the vent valve is in the SEALING position. Using the display panel, select the MANUAL/PRESSURE COOK function and HIGH PRESSURE, and use the +/− buttons until the display reads 10 minutes.

5. When the cooker beeps to let you know it's finished, let it naturally come down in pressure until the display reads LO:10. Switch the vent valve from the SEALING to the VENTING position. Use caution while the steam escapes—it's hot.

6. Serve the cobbler warm with your favorite dairy-free ice cream or coconut whipped cream.

COCONUT WHIPPED CREAM

I keep a can of coconut milk in the refrigerator at all times so I can make coconut whipped cream whenever the need arises. This is a great dairy-free replacement for the fluffy whip that everyone loves.

1 (15-ounce) can full-fat coconut milk

1½ teaspoons 100% pure maple syrup

¼ teaspoon pure vanilla extract

Refrigerate the can of coconut milk for 8 hours or overnight. Open the can and carefully scoop ½ cup of the solidified cream from the top of the can and place it inside a medium bowl (see Note). Add the maple syrup and vanilla extract. Use a hand mixer with a whisk attachment to beat the cream until fluffy like whipped cream. Store in the refrigerator for up to 3 days.

Note: Use the leftover coconut milk in smoothies, coconut rice, or recipes that call for milk.

CHEWY CHOCOLATE CHIP COOKIES

It seems like every grain-free cookie out there is made with almond or coconut flour, but I like to use buckwheat flour. Don't let the name scare you off, buckwheat is actually a seed that is high in protein and fiber! These cookies are allergy friendly too, as I use tahini instead of peanut butter. Tahini is a seed butter that comes from blending oil and roasted sesame seeds. Allergic to eggs? No problem! These cookies work well with Flax Eggs (page 229). To make these even better, I use Enjoy Life brand mini chocolate chips. They are vegan, allergy-friendly chocolate chips that taste just as delicious as Nestlé chips.

MAKES 18 COOKIES

¾ cup tahini (page 267 or store-bought), almond, peanut, or sunflower seed butter

½ cup buckwheat flour

1 teaspoon baking soda

½ cup 100% pure maple syrup

1 large egg

½ cup dairy-free mini chocolate chips

1. Preheat the oven to 350°F. Linc a large baking sheet with parchment paper (see Note).

2. Combine the tahini, buckwheat flour, baking soda, maple syrup, and egg in a food processor. Process until well combined, 10 to 15 seconds. Stir in the chocolate chips.

3. Using a 1½-tablespoon cookie scoop, portion the dough onto the prepared baking sheet, arranging the cookies about ½ inch apart. Bake for 10 to 12 minutes, until the cookies are very lightly browned. Let cool slightly, then transfer to a rack to cool completely. Store in an airtight container at room temperature for 3 days.

Note: For an extra boost of protein, add a tablespoon of collagen peptides.

Note: Dark baking sheets will give you a dark color on the bottom of the cookies, I recommend using a light-colored baking sheet or stainless steel.

STRAWBERRY SHORTCAKE MINIS

These cute little mini biscuits are the perfect sized after-dinner dessert! With just the right amount of sweetness in each biscuit filled with lightly sweetened berries, they can be addicting.

MAKES 8 TO 10 SHORTCAKES

FOR THE BISCUITS

2 large eggs

1 cup tightly packed superfine blanched almond flour

1 tablespoon avocado oil

1 tablespoon raw honey

½ teaspoon pure vanilla extract

¼ teaspoon fine sea salt

½ teaspoon coconut sugar

FOR THE STRAWBERRY FILLING

16 strawberries, quartered

2 tablespoons raw honey

Coconut Whipped Cream (page 294), optional

1. Preheat the oven to 350°F. Line a baking sheet with parchment paper.

2. For the biscuits: Combine the eggs, almond flour, avocado oil, honey, vanilla, and sea salt in a food processor and process until combined.

3. Using a 1½-tablespoon cookie scoop, portion the dough onto the prepared baking sheet, arranging the biscuits about ½ inch apart. Sprinkle the tops with a little coconut sugar.

4. Bake for 15 to 20 minutes, until the biscuits are lightly browned and cooked through, then leave them in the pan to cool slightly.

5. While the biscuits are baking, prepare the filling: Combine the strawberries and honey in a bowl and stir.

6. After the biscuits have cooled slightly, cut them in half using a bread knife. Fill with strawberries and top with coconut whipped cream, if desired.

STRAWBERRY-COCONUT MOUSSE

Light and airy, this mousse is great served as an after-dinner treat soon after being made—or place in the freezer to enjoy as an ice cream later.

10 frozen strawberries

½ cup coconut cream

1½ teaspoons raw honey

¼ teaspoon pure vanilla extract

Place all of the ingredients in a high-powered blender and blend on high until smooth. Serve immediately, or freeze for 2 hours for a more solidified, scoopable ice cream texture.

THE PERFECT PUMPKIN PIE

If you follow me on Instagram, you know that it took me a bazillion-and-one tries to get this pie just right. When I got it though, man did I get it! Last Thanksgiving, hundreds of people around the country, plus a few from other parts of the world, made this pie for the holiday. I wasn't surprised when I received nothing but rave reviews. The recipe is for a mini pie though, so if you are cooking for a crowd, you'll want to double the recipe and bake it in a 9-inch pie pan in a conventional oven at 350°F for 35 to 40 minutes. I hope your family loves it just as much as mine does!

––––––––––––––––––––––––––––––– **SERVES 6 TO 8** –––––––––––––––––––––––––––––––

2 tablespoons salted butter or ghee, plus some for greasing

1 large egg, white and yolk separated

½ cup plus 1 tablespoon arrowroot flour

½ cup superfine blanched almond flour, tightly packed

¼ teaspoon fine sea salt

1 cup canned organic pumpkin puree

¼ cup 100% pure maple syrup

1½ teaspoons pumpkin pie spice

1 cup water

Coconut Whipped Cream (page 294)

1. Grease a 6-cup baking dish that fits inside your electric pressure cooker with butter or ghee. (A 7-inch circular, oven-safe dish should work for this recipe.) Combine the 2 tablespoons butter, the egg white, ½ cup of the arrowroot flour, the almond flour, and sea salt in a food processor. Process on high until the mixture turns into a crumbly dough, about 15 seconds.

2. Press the dough firmly into the prepared baking dish along the bottom and creeping up the sides of the dish, as a pie crust. Set aside.

3. Combine the remaining 1 tablespoon arrowroot flour, the pumpkin puree, maple syrup, egg yolk, and pumpkin pie spice in the food processor. Process until combined, about 10 seconds. Pour the pumpkin mixture in the pie crust, cover the dish with foil, and place on top of the trivet.

4. Pour 1 cup water into the pressure cooker and carefully lower the trivet and dish into the pot. Place the lid on the cooker and make sure the vent valve is in the SEALING position. Using the display panel, select the MANUAL/PRESSURE COOK function and HIGH PRESSURE, and use the +/− buttons until the display reads 30 minutes.

5. When the cooker beeps to let you know it's finished, switch the vent valve from the SEALING to the VENTING position, administering a quick release. Use caution while the steam escapes—it's hot.

6. Remove the pie from the pot and uncover. Let sit for 15 minutes before serving with coconut whipped cream. Keeps in the refrigerator for up to 1 week.

SNICKERDOODLES

Cinnamon sugar cookies, does it get better than that? Because I had so many almond flour–based cookies in the first book, it was important to me to create a few cookie recipes that were a bit more allergy friendly. These are still grain free and just as delicious, but made with seeds instead of nuts!

MAKES 18 COOKIES

½ cup buckwheat flour

1 teaspoon baking soda

1 large egg

¾ cup tahini (page 267 or store-bought)

½ cup 100% pure maple syrup

1 tablespoon collagen peptides (optional)

2 teaspoons ground cinnamon

2 teaspoons coconut sugar

1. Preheat the oven to 350°F. Line large baking sheet with parchment paper.

2. Combine the buckwheat flour, baking soda, egg, tahini, maple syrup, and collagen peptides, if desired, in a food processor. Process on high until well combined, 10 to 15 seconds.

3. In a separate bowl, mix together the cinnamon and coconut sugar.

4. Using a 1½-tablespoon cookie scoop, portion the dough onto the prepared baking sheet, arranging the balls about ½ inch apart. Sprinkle each ball with cinnamon sugar.

5. Bake the cookies for 10 to 12 minutes, until very lightly browned. Let cool slightly and transfer each cookie to a rack to cool completely. Store in an airtight container at room temperature, or enjoy one now and freeze the rest for later.

MAPLE PECAN PIE

Traditionally, pecan pie is made with loads of corn syrup. We've chosen not to eat that kind of sugar anymore. Instead, we've started making our pecan pies with maple syrup and applesauce for sweetness. This is a mini pie recipe. If you're serving a large group of people, you'll want to double the recipe and bake it in a 9-inch pie pan in a conventional oven at 350°F for 35 to 40 minutes.

SERVES 6 TO 8

---

2 tablespoons salted butter or ghee, plus some for greasing

1 large egg, white and yolk separated

½ cup plus 1 tablespoon arrowroot flour

½ cup tightly packed superfine blanched almond flour

¼ teaspoon plus ⅛ teaspoon fine sea salt

¼ cup 100% pure maple syrup

¼ cup unsweetened applesauce

1 teaspoon ground cinnamon

⅛ teaspoon baking soda

1½ cups raw pecan halves

1 cup water

1. Grease a 6-cup baking dish that fits inside your electric pressure cooker with butter or ghee. (A 7-inch circular, oven-safe dish should work for this recipe.)

2. Combine the 2 tablespoons butter, the egg white, ½ cup of the arrowroot flour, the almond flour, and ¼ teaspoon of the sea salt in a food processor. Process on high until the mixture turns into a crumbly dough, about 15 seconds.

3. Press the dough firmly into the prepared baking dish along the bottom and creeping up the sides of the dish, as a pie crust. Set aside.

4. Combine the egg yolk, maple syrup, applesauce, cinnamon, baking soda, remaining 1 tablespoon arrowroot flour, and remaining ⅛ teaspoon sea salt in the food processor. Process until combined, about 10 seconds. Stir in the pecan halves and then pour the mixture into the pie crust. Cover the dish with foil and place on top of the trivet.

5. Pour 1 cup water into the pressure cooker and carefully lower the trivet and dish into the pot. Place the lid on the cooker and make sure the vent valve is in the SEALING position. Using the display panel, select the MANUAL/PRESSURE COOK function and HIGH PRESSURE, and use the +/− buttons until the display reads 30 minutes.

6. When the cooker beeps to let you know it's finished, switch the vent valve from the SEALING to the VENTING position, administering a quick release. Use caution while the steam escapes—it's hot.

7. Remove the pie from the pot and uncover. Let sit for 15 minutes before serving. Keep in the refrigerator for up to 1 week.

BUCKEYES

Chocolate-covered peanut butter balls, just let that sink in. . . . Basically, it's a classic peanut butter cup made to look like the nut from Ohio's state tree. These yummy little treats are great for snacking or dessert. My mouth is watering just thinking about them!

MAKES 8

¼ cup plus 1 tablespoon salted butter or ghee

¼ cup organic peanut, almond, or sunflower seed butter

1 cup PBfit peanut butter powder

¼ cup agave nectar or 100% pure maple syrup

½ teaspoon pure vanilla extract

⅛ teaspoon fine sea salt

¼ cup dairy-free chocolate chips

1. In a saucepan, melt ¼ cup of the butter and the peanut butter over medium-high heat and stir to combine. Remove from the heat and whisk in the peanut butter powder, agave, vanilla extract, and salt.

2. Form the mixture into eight balls with a 1-tablespoon cookie scoop and place on a plate lined with parchment paper.

3. In a small pot over medium-high heat, combine the remaining 1 tablespoon butter and the chocolate chips. Whisk continuously until melted. Remove from the heat. Using your hand, carefully dip the bottom of each peanut butter ball into the chocolate and set, chocolate side down, on the plate.

4. Refrigerate the cookies for 1 hour, until the chocolate sets, then serve. Store leftovers in the refrigerator for up to 2 weeks.

JAM THUMBPRINT COOKIES

My number 1 favorite cookie, ever, is the jam thumbprint cookie. When I was a kid, my mom got a special Christmas cookie edition of *Better Homes and Gardens* magazine. Inside were these gorgeous thumbprint cookies. I begged Mom to let me try to make them for Christmas. She agreed and everyone *oohed* and *ahhed* over the finished result. After that success, they became my Christmas thing and I've made them every year since. As you can imagine, the recipe scrap from that magazine is pretty worn out now. In 2017, when we went gluten-free, I got creative and came up with a new thumbprint cookie recipe: no white sugar, no wheat flour, and only eight ingredients, because sometimes simple is best. It's my honor to share this recipe, which is so close and special to my heart, with you. I hope they become a Christmas staple in your home as well.

To change things up, spread peanut butter over the top for a PB&J cookie!

MAKES 12 COOKIES

1 large egg

1½ cups tightly packed superfine blanched almond flour

½ teaspoon baking soda

¼ teaspoon fine sea salt

2 tablespoons 100% pure maple syrup

1 teaspoon salted butter or ghee

½ teaspoon almond extract

6 teaspoons strawberry jam or Blueberry Jam (page 265)

1. Preheat the oven to 350°F. Line a large baking sheet with parchment paper.

2. Combine the egg, almond flour, baking soda, sea salt, maple syrup, butter, and almond extract in a stand mixer. Blend on medium-high until a dough combines and forms a ball. If you don't have a stand mixer, you can mix by hand in a large bowl.

3. Using a 1½-tablespoon cookie scoop, portion the dough onto the prepared baking sheet, arranging the cookies ½ inch apart. Lightly press your thumb into the center of each rounded ball to form a small indentation.

4. Use a ½-teaspoon measuring spoon to fill each thumbprint with jam, being careful to not overfill.

5. Bake the cookies for 12 minutes, until the cookies have darkened in color slightly. Let cool slightly on the baking sheet before serving. Store in an airtight container at room temperature for up to 2 days.

COOKIE DOUGH POPS

I make these and stick them in the freezer for times of crisis. You know, those moments where you just need something sweet or you're going to explode? Those times. We all have those desperate moments when we make poor choices because we're hungry, having cravings, or are just flat-out emotional. Having a little treat like this on hand makes managing those moments a little bit easier.

MAKES 6 (3-OUNCE) POPS

1 cup water

1 cup raw cashews

⅓ cup 100% pure maple syrup

1½ tablespoons tahini
(page 267 or store-bought)

1½ teaspoons pure vanilla
extract

¼ teaspoon fine sea salt

2 tablespoons dairy-free mini
chocolate chips

1. Combine the water, cashews, maple syrup, tahini, vanilla, and sea salt in a high-powered blender. Blend on high until the ingredients are completely blended, about 45 seconds. Add the chocolate chips and pulse three times.

2. Use the dough to fill 6 (3-ounce) popsicle molds and freeze for 1 hour or overnight. The pops keep in the freezer for up to 2 weeks.

CARAMEL POPCORN

I have a big weakness for sweets. This caramel popcorn is so good and so very easy to put together. It's way better than any commercial brand. Popcorn is inexpensive, which is why I always have some kernels in the pantry. Feel free to add roasted nuts or chocolate chips once the popcorn cools. Beware, this stuff is addicting!

— **MAKES 4 CUPS** —

¼ cup 100% maple syrup

4 tablespoons salted butter or ghee

⅛ teaspoon fine sea salt

6 cups popped popcorn (from ¼ cup kernels)

1. Combine the maple syrup, butter, and sea salt in a small saucepan and bring to a boil. Boil for 1 minute, stirring continuously with a wooden spoon. Place the popped popcorn in a large bowl. Pour the caramel mixture over the popcorn and stir to coat.

2. Transfer the popcorn to a 5.3-quart air fryer basket and bake for 25 minutes at 200°F, stirring once halfway through (see Note).

3. When the air fryer beeps to signal that it's finished, carefully release the basket from the housing and shake the popcorn onto a baking sheet to cool. Once cooled, store the popcorn at room temperature in an airtight container or glass jar for up to a week.

Note: To bake the popcorn in a conventional oven, transfer the coated popcorn to a baking sheet lined with parchment paper. Bake in a 250°F oven for 45 minutes, stirring twice. Let the popcorn cool before storing.

index